Low-Mess Crafts for KIDS

Paper Roll Octopus (page 34)

Low-Mess Crafts for KIDS

≥72 Projects to Create Your Own Magical Worlds

DEBBIE CHAPMAN

founder of
One Little Project

PAGE STREET
PUBLISHING CO.

PAGE STREET
PUBLISHING CO.

First published in 2018 by

Page Street Publishing Co.

27 Congress Street, Suite 105

Salem, MA 01970

www.pagestreetpublishing.com

Distributed by Macmillan, sales in Canada by The Canadian Manda Group.

22   21   20   19   18   1   2   3   4   5

ISBN-13: 978-1-62414-558-2

ISBN-10: 1-62414-558-2

Library of Congress Control Number: 2017956927

Cover and book design by Page Street Publishing Co.

Photography by Debbie Chapman

Cover images: *Fuzzy Friend Sock Puppet (page 90), Paper Roll Giraffe (page 80), Plastic Cup Whale (page 44), Plastic Spoon Mermaid (page 38), Pipe Cleaner Finger Puppets (page 102)*

Printed and bound in China

> For my little creators <
LEAH, KATE and BENJAMIN

My Secret GARDEN

Under THE SEA

Summer at THE BEACH

Painted Sea Turtles (page 48)

HELLO FELLOW CRAFTERS

I'm Debbie Chapman, author and owner of the website One Little Project. This book has been a labor of love, and I am so excited to share it with you!

I love crafts. And I love creating things with my kids—who, coincidentally, also love crafts. But boy can my kids make a mess! And I'm pretty sure they're not the only messy kids out there. So I've put together 72 of the cutest and the most fun kids crafts that you can make at home—with as little mess as possible!

Crafting with kids can be overwhelming sometimes. It can be just. So. Messy. But it doesn't have to be. Of course, it really depends on the child and what you're making, but the crafts in this book will help keep messes, splatters, spills, and scraps from getting in the way of having fun.

This book is all about making things that you can actually play with. There is no artwork to hang on the fridge here, just really awesome objects that you can make at home with simple materials.

The crafts in each chapter of this book stick to a theme and if you make all of them within a chapter, you can put them together in a fun little scene. Then you can play with the amazing things you just created. How cool is that?! There's even a list of supplies for each entire chapter at the end of the book to make it easier to gather everything you'll need.

Or you can simply pick and choose a craft and make it on its own. The best thing about crafting is that you get to decide! So go ahead and start creating things, one little project at a time.

For even more fun ideas you can visit my website at onelittleproject.com.

Happy crafting!

—DEBBIE

BUILDING UP YOUR CRAFT STASH ✦⁺

I bought most of the craft supplies used in this book from my local craft store and dollar stores. If you have trouble finding something in stores, don't forget to check online. I recommend Amazon.com; it has a great selection of inexpensive craft supplies!

Don't worry one bit if you don't have the exact material listed in a craft. Part of the fun of making things is thinking of fun and creative alternatives. I bet there are tons of things in your home that you never would have thought of using for crafts (especially in the recycling bin!). Be creative and see what kinds of solutions you can come up with as you go.

It can be tough to know what supplies are best to stock up on for crafts. Here's a little list to help you get started. To see a complete list of supplies for each chapter, see page 176.

These are the crafting supplies that my kids and I use most often. Try to build up a collection of these items in lots of different colors and sizes

- Construction paper
- Thick colored paper
- Pipe cleaners
- Googly eyes
- Craft sticks
- Sticker rhinestones
- Pom poms

And here's a list of the most useful crafting tools that you'll need

- White glue
- Low-temperature glue gun
- Glue stick
- Crafter's tape
- Transparent tape
- Masking tape
- Washable markers
- Pencil
- Gel pen (black)
- Single hole punch
- Paint brushes
- Scissors

Pipe Cleaner Flower Fairy (page 18)

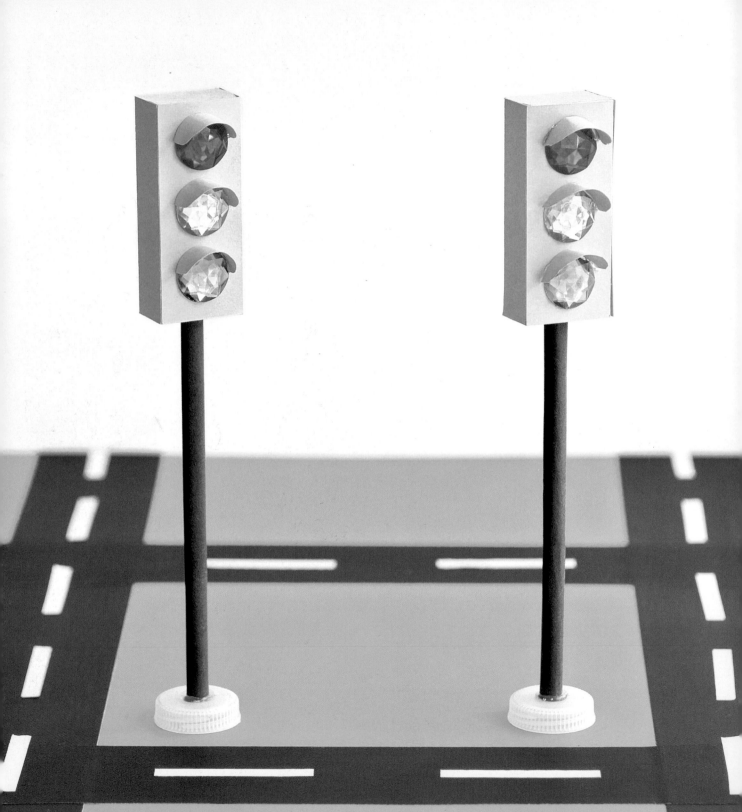

Candy Box Traffic Lights (page 108), Poster Board Road Track (page 118)

GLUE GUNS AND KIDS
A NOTE TO GROWNUPS...

As you flip through this book, you'll notice that I recommend using a glue gun for some of the crafts. Some materials are stubborn and really do need a little bit of extra sticking power that white glue just can't handle. I recently discovered that you could buy low-temperature glue guns, which tend to be a lot safer for kids to use. They are usually inexpensive and they're a great tool to keep in your crafting supply stash!

Low-temperature glue guns aren't as hot as regular glue guns, and they are often much smaller in size, which makes them much more manageable for kids to use. The metal tip isn't as hot as a regular glue gun, but it is quite hot, so you still need to be careful.

Make sure you read the packaging and explain to your child how to properly use a glue gun. Remind them that you can't touch the metal tip where the glue comes out and you can't touch the glue until it's dry.

My kids have been using glue guns (with me close by) since they were 3 years old without any issues—and that was before I knew about the low-temperature ones. Every child is different and only you know how responsible your child will be, so please help or monitor them as you need to while the glue gun is being used. They will be thrilled that you trust them with the responsibility!

Chapter 1

My Secret GARDEN

Create a family of your own magical flower fairies to live in this special secret garden, created all by you! In this chapter you'll find glowing fairy houses (page 16), sparkling dragonflies (page 24) and enchanted toadstools (page 30). Don't forget the most important part—the secret door that leads from our world into your new mystical garden!

⩔ LOW-MESS TIP: KEEP IT SIMPLE ⩔

Choosing crafts that use very few materials is the easiest way to keep an activity low-mess. After all, the less you take out, the less you'll have to put away when you're done!

Most of the crafts in this chapter only use a handful of materials, which makes it easy to tidy them up when you're done! This is especially true for the Folded Paper Butterflies (page 28)—you'll only need 3 things to make those! It's amazing what you can create with just a few simple supplies!

Paper Roll Fairy House (page 16), Pipe Cleaner Flower Fairy (page 18), Simple Paper Daisies (page 20), Craft Stick Fairy Door (page 22), Sparkly Pom Pom Dragonflies (page 24), Folded Paper Pine Trees (page 26), Folded Paper Butterflies (page 28), Painted Rock Toadstools (page 30)

Paper Roll Fairy House

LEVEL OF DIFFICULTY 3/5 ◆
PARENTAL SUPERVISION—ASK A GROWN UP TO HELP WITH THE GLUE GUN.

THE BEST PART ABOUT THESE FAIRY HOUSES is that you can make them any color you like—and I definitely recommend trying lots of colors. But forget about pulling out lots of messy paint colors—just use colored paper instead! You'll end up with a brightly colored fairy village and the only thing you'll be left with is a few scraps of paper. (I like to save those scraps for future creations!)

OUT OF EVERY CRAFT IN THIS BOOK, these were my daughters' favorite! They spent hours playing with their little fairy village. They absolutely loved that the light from the tea lights makes the windows light up. Most battery operated tea lights flicker a little, so it's fun to imagine a tiny little fairy fluttering around inside!

MATERIALS
- 2 pieces thick colored paper (any color)
- 1 piece printer paper (white)
- 3 to 5 small rhinestone stickers
- Battery-operated tea light

TOOLS
- Scissors
- Pencil
- Tape
- Washable markers
- Low-temperature glue gun

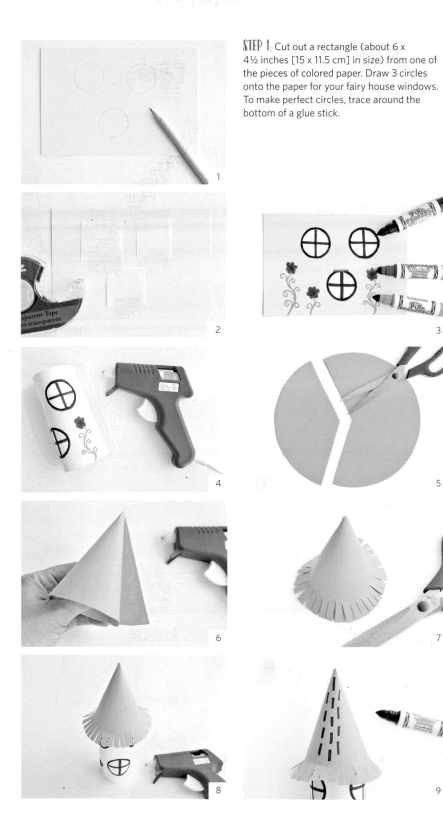

STEP 1: Cut out a rectangle (about 6 x 4½ inches [15 x 11.5 cm] in size) from one of the pieces of colored paper. Draw 3 circles onto the paper for your fairy house windows. To make perfect circles, trace around the bottom of a glue stick.

STEP 2: Carefully use the point of the scissors to poke a hole in the middle of each circle, then cut out the window holes. Cut out squares of white printer paper, just slightly larger than the window holes. Place a paper square so that it covers each window and tape it in place.

STEP 3: Flip the paper rectangle back to the front and use washable markers to decorate your fairy house with flowers and vines. Press a small rhinestone sticker onto the center of each flower.

STEP 4: Roll the paper rectangle into a tube shape. Place a piece of tape on the inside of the tube to hold it in place. Squeeze a line of hot glue along the edge of the colored paper, then carefully pinch it closed.

STEP 5: Using a pencil, trace around the edge of a large round plate on the other piece of colored paper, then cut out the circle with your scissors. Cut out a one-third wedge (as if you were cutting a piece of pie) from the circle.

STEP 6: Roll the wedge of paper around itself to make a cone shape. The bottom of the cone should be just larger than the paper tube you just made. Place a piece of tape on the inside of the cone to hold it together while you glue. Run a line of hot glue close to the edge of the paper and pinch it closed.

STEP 7: Cut a fringe around the bottom edge of the cone by snipping ½-inch (1.3-cm) cuts around the entire edge, straight up towards the point of the cone.

STEP 8: Squeeze a line of hot glue around the top edge of the paper tube. Gently press the cone roof onto the house, making sure the seams line up at the back.

STEP 9: Using a black washable marker, draw straight dashed lines, all the way around, from the point of the cone down towards the fringe.

Turn on your battery operated tea light and place your paper roll house on top of it. Turn off the lights and watch the windows glow!

Your paper roll fairy house is complete!

Pipe Cleaner Flower Fairy

LEVEL OF DIFFICULTY 5/5 ♦ PARENTAL SUPERVISION NOT REQUIRED.

IT REALLY IS AMAZING what you can make when you add fabric flowers to your stash of craft supplies. These flower fairies are beautiful and they are really simple to make. And best of all, when you're all finished, you'll only be left with one small pipe cleaner scrap. What an easy clean up!

I'M NOT THE BEST when it comes to drawing, so faces always make me a little nervous. But my best advice is just to keep the faces simple. Don't try to make the face complicated and don't add too many features. Little circles for eyes and a little curve for the mouth are all you need to make a happy and adorable face.

MATERIALS
- 1 fabric gerbera daisy flower
- 1 craft stick
- 4 pipe cleaners (3 pink and 1 light brown)
- 2 sparkly pipe cleaners (pink)
- 1" (2.5-cm) wooden bead

TOOLS
- Scissors
- Washable markers (red and black)
- White glue or low-temperature glue gun

STEP 1: Remove the plastic end piece that holds together the fabric flower. Slide the large flower piece onto the craft stick. Use scissors to cut a slightly larger opening in the middle of the flowers, if needed, to make it fit.

STEP 2: Fold the light brown pipe cleaner in half to find the middle. Open it back up and place the middle of the pipe cleaner behind the craft stick. Take the left end of the pipe cleaner and wrap it around all the way to the right. Take the right end of the pipe cleaner and wrap it around all the way to the left. Twist, then bring each end back to the middle.

1

2

3

5

7

9

4

6

8

10

STEP 3: Bend the pipe cleaner forward near the end on each side to make hands and bend it forward again near the middles to make elbows.

Wind one of the pink pipe cleaners around the craft stick over and around the brown pipe cleaner to hold the arms in place. Then wind it tightly around the craft stick below the arms to make the fairy's waist.

STEP 4: Fold the second pink pipe cleaner in half. Fold each end back to the center fold to make a "W" shape. Pinch the folds closed to make two fairy legs. Bend up the ends of the legs to make feet.

STEP 5: Place the fairy legs under the fabric flower. Starting about 1 inch (2.5 cm) above the fairy's feet, wind the third pink pipe cleaner tightly around the legs and the craft stick to hold it in place. Keep winding upwards, towards the fabric flower, until you run out of pipe cleaner.

STEP 6: Using washable markers, draw a simple face on the wooden bead. Push the wooden bead onto the top of the craft stick.

STEP 7: Squeeze a small line of white glue around the opening at the top of the wooden bead. Insert the center part of the fabric flower into the top of the wooden bead and gently press it against the glue to hold it in place. Allow the glue to dry.

STEP 8: To make the fairy wings, follow Step 1 to Step 5 of the Sparkly Pom Pom Dragonflies (page 24) using the 2 sparkly pipe cleaners. Shape them into fairy wings by gently opening each pipe cleaner loop.

STEP 9: Squeeze a small glob of glue onto the back of the fairy behind the arms. Gently press the fairy wings onto the white glue. Allow the glue to dry.

STEP 10: Your pipe cleaner flower fairy is complete!

HINT: Paint pens and permanent markers will bleed if you use them on a wooden bead. If you have trouble with your ink bleeding, use your finger to add a thin layer of white glue to the wooden bead and allow it to dry before you draw the face.

Simple Paper Daisies

LEVEL OF DIFFICULTY 4/5 ✦ PARENTAL SUPERVISION NOT REQUIRED

MATERIALS
- 1 scrap of paper, 3 x 8½" (7.5 x 21.5-cm) wide
- 1 large rhinestone sticker
- 1 craft stick (green)
- 1 pipe cleaner (green)

TOOLS
- Scissors
- Glue stick
- White glue or low-temperature glue gun

I ABSOLUTELY LOVE FLOWER CRAFTS. I live in Canada, so by the end of winter I'm usually so excited for the warm weather to come that I end up crafting all sorts of flowers while I wait for my spring bulbs to bloom. Especially if there's still snow on the ground!

THESE DAISY SHAPED FLOWERS LOOK SO BEAUTIFUL. They use only a handful of supplies and leave almost no scraps behind when you're done. In fact, these flowers are an awesome way to use up leftover paper scraps from other creations you've made.

STEP 1: Cut 16 strips of paper, approximately ⅜ x 3 inches (1 x 7.5 cm) long. Using a glue stick, glue the ends of the paper strips together to make petals (don't fold the ends). If you've used heavier paper, you might need white glue or a hot glue gun to keep them from popping open.

STEP 2: Place a large rhinestone sticker with the sticky side facing up on a flat surface. Press the end of one of the petals onto the sticky part of the rhinestone so the curved end points straight outwards.

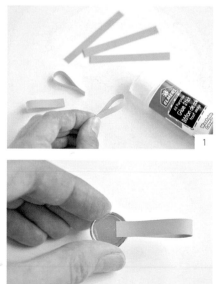

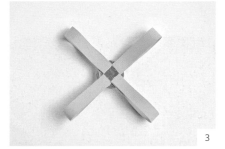

3

4

5

6

7

8

9

10

STEP 3 : Add 3 more petals to the back of the rhinestone sticker to make an X shape.

STEP 4: Add 4 more petals to the back of the rhinestone, spacing them evenly between the petals you've already added. If the sticky part of the rhinestone is covered, use a glue stick to keep them in place. If you're using heavier paper, use white glue or a hot glue gun to keep them in place.

STEP 5: Glue on the remaining 8 petals to fill in the gaps. Turn the flower right side up. Gently bend each of the petals slightly upwards around the rhinestone.

STEP 6: Using white glue or a glue gun, attach the green craft stick to the back of the flower. Allow it to dry.

STEP 7: Cross the ends of the green pipe cleaner slightly and twist the ends around themselves to make a circle shape.

STEP 8: Bring the opposite sides of the circle together and pinch the ends to fold them.

STEP 9: Slide the craft stick through the middle of the pipe cleaner. Twist the pipe cleaner tightly on both sides of the craft stick to hold it in place. Gently pull apart the folded pipe cleaner to make a leaf shape on both sides of the popsicle stick. Bend the leaves upwards slightly towards the flower.

STEP 10: Your simple paper flower is complete!

HINT: If you're making this craft with younger kids, you can make it quick and easy by using fewer strips of paper and making them wide instead of thin.

Craft Stick Fairy Door

MATERIALS
- 8 colored craft sticks
- 1 button

TOOLS
- White glue
- Scissors

LEVEL OF DIFFICULTY 2/5 ◆ PARENTAL SUPERVISION
ASK A GROWN UP TO HELP WITH CUTTING THE CRAFT STICKS.

THERE'S NOTHING MORE MAGICAL than imagining your very own bedroom somehow connecting with another world. And every secret garden needs to have a door! My daughters like to lean their fairy doors against the wall in their bedroom and pretend that the fairies can come through them.

KEEP THE MESS DOWN by using colored craft sticks instead of painting them. You can make your door any color of the rainbow and you can even adjust the shape. Maybe yours will be curved on top? Or square? Or maybe it's so rickety that it's nearly falling apart? Just make sure you remember to find something extra special in your craft stash to use as the door knob.

STEP 1: Using a sharp pair of scissors, carefully cut one of the craft sticks in half.

STEP 2: Cut a second craft stick at an angle so that it is approximately 3½ inches (9 cm) long at the longest point.

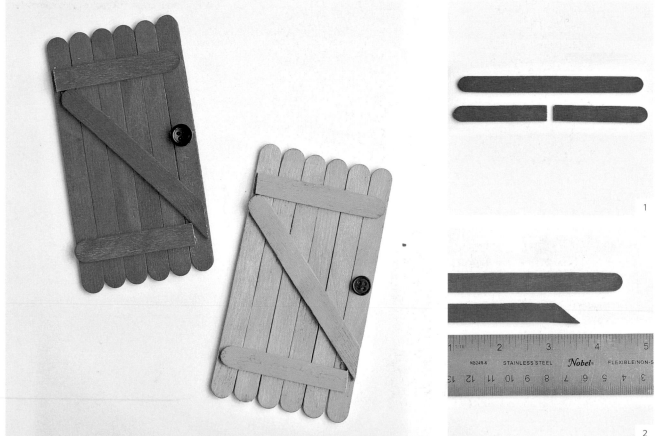

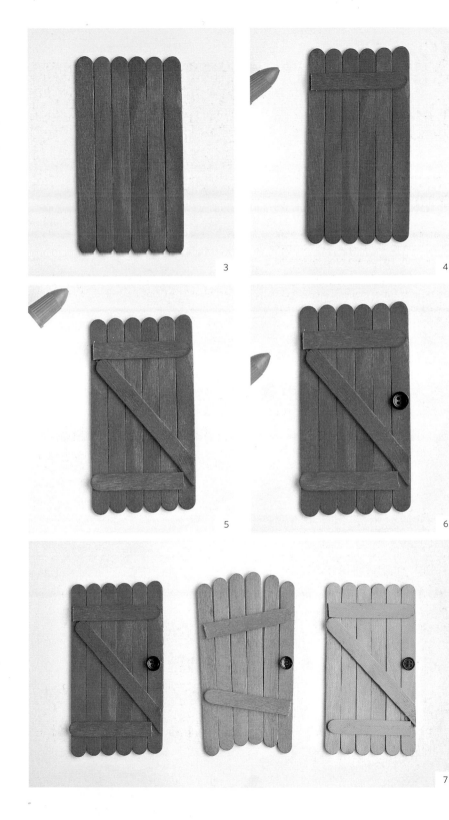

STEP 3: Place 6 craft sticks side by side on a flat and even surface, lining up the top and bottom edges so they are even.

STEP 4: Squeeze a line of white glue along one side of the craft stick halves and gently press it onto the 6 lined up craft sticks, about ½ inch (1.3 cm) from the top.

STEP 5: Squeeze a line of white glue along one side of the craft stick that was cut on an angle and gently press it onto the 6 lined up craft sticks at an angle. Finally, squeeze a line of white glue along one side of the other craft stick half and gently press it onto the 6 lined up craft sticks, about ½ inch (1.3 cm) from the bottom.

STEP 6: Squeeze a small glob of glue onto the back of a button. Gently press the button onto the craft stick door to make a door knob. Allow the glue to dry.

STEP 7: Your craft stick fairy door is complete!

✦ Sparkly Pom Pom ✦ Dragonflies

LEVEL OF DIFFICULTY 3/5 ✦ PARENTAL SUPERVISION
ASK A GROWNUP TO HELP WITH THE GLUE GUN.

HAVE YOU EVER SEEN A REAL DRAGONFLY fluttering over a pond? They are usually shimmery green, blue or red, and they really do sparkle! These dragonflies remind me of the ones I used to see in my backyard when I was a kid.

FORGET ABOUT USING GLITTER FOR THIS ONE. just use materials that sparkle and shine all on their own! Try using sticker rhinestones, or sparkly foam circle stickers to bring your dragonflies to life. You can clip these sparkly little creatures onto your books, your backpack or even onto your clothes. Then watch them shimmer in the sunlight, just like real dragonflies!

MATERIALS
- 2 sparkly pipe cleaners
- 1 clothespin
- 5 medium sparkly pom poms
- 1 large sparkly pom pom
- 2 small googly eyes

TOOLS
- Scissors
- Crafter's tape
- Low-temperature glue gun

STEP 1: Keep one pipe cleaner at its full length. Trim off approximately 2½ inches (6.5 cm) from the second pipe cleaner.

STEP 2: Take the ends of one of the pipe cleaners and cross them slightly.

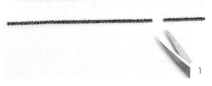

3

4

STEP 3: Twist the ends to make a circle shape. Repeat for both pipe cleaners.

STEP 4: Bring the opposite ends of the pipe cleaner circle together until they meet in the middle. Twist it a couple of times. Repeat for the second pipe cleaner circle.

STEP 5: Bend the wings slightly towards one side to finish the wings.

STEP 6: Attach the googly eyes to the large pom pom using crafter's tape.

STEP 7: Add a small glob of hot glue to the end of the clothespin and carefully press the large pom pom onto the glue with the eyes pointing towards the front.

STEP 8: Add a small glob of hot glue just behind the large pom pom and attach the large set of wings so that the wings point towards the front. Add a small glob of hot glue right on top of the middle of the large wings and attach the small set of wings so that the small wings point towards the back.

STEP 9: Add a small glob of hot glue as close to the wings as possible and attach one of the medium pom poms. Continue gluing the medium pom poms onto the clothespin using hot glue until you reach the end of the clothespin.

STEP 10: Your sparkly pom pom dragonfly is complete!

5

6

7

8

9

10

Folded Paper Pine Trees

LEVEL OF DIFFICULTY 3/5 ✦ PARENTAL SUPERVISION NOT REQUIRED.

MATERIALS
- 1 piece of construction paper (green)
- 1 toothpick
- 1 wine cork

TOOLS
- Pencil
- Scissors
- Glue stick
- Tape

I'VE ALWAYS WANTED to be able to make those fancy little paper ballerinas. The ones that you make out of folded paper so that when you unfold them you have an amazing garland of ballerinas that look like they are holding hands. But, every time I try to make them, I end up with 4 or 5 ballerinas that are completely unattached. So these trees are perfect and so much simpler, since the idea is to make 4 identical, but completely unattached tree shapes.

THIS IS AN EASY CRAFT TO KEEP TIDY. Just remember to only pull out one sheet of construction paper at a time and make sure you use a glue stick and tape instead of liquid glue to hold your creation together. Besides being low-mess, you don't have to wait for anything to dry!

STEP 1: Fold the construction paper in half along the long edge. Open up the paper, then bring one of the long edges to the center. Press along the edge to create a fold.

STEP 2: Bring the other long edge to the center and create a fold.

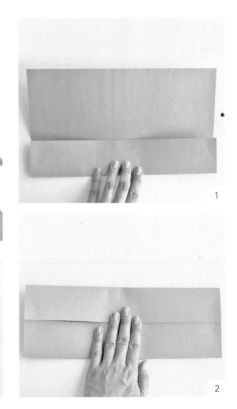

STEP 3: Fold the paper in half to make a long, thin rectangle.

STEP 4: Fold the long rectangle in half one last time to make a shorter rectangle. Using a pencil, draw the shape of half a pine tree. Make sure the middle of the tree is along the side with 4 folded edges. Keeping the paper folded, carefully cut out the tree shape along the pencil line.

STEP 5: You'll end up with 4 identical tree shapes.

STEP 6: Fold one of the tree shapes in half, then use a glue stick to apply glue to the top surface.

STEP 7: Line up the second tree shape over the top of the surface with the glue, and press the pieces together so that the branches line up. Add more glue with the glue stick and attach the third and fourth tree shapes following the same method.

STEP 8: Place the toothpick in the center fold, leaving about ½ inch (1.3 cm) coming out at the bottom. Hold it in place with a piece of tape. Use a glue stick to apply glue to the entire open surface of the tree. Carefully line up the branches of the tree and pinch it closed.

STEP 9: Carefully press the toothpick into the end of the wine cork. If you're having trouble getting the toothpick into the wine cork, try using a small screw and a screwdriver to make a hole first.

Step 10: Your folded paper pine tree is complete!

> **HINT:** If you have the time and patience, I recommend cutting out even more than 4 tree shapes because the more pieces you glue into your tree, the cooler it will end up looking!

Folded Paper Butterflies

LEVEL OF DIFFICULTY 4/5 ✦ PARENTAL SUPERVISION NOT REQUIRED

THIS FLUTTERY FAMILY OF BUTTERFLIES is beautiful and so simple to make. This isn't officially origami because we'll be cutting the paper, but it's a great way to practice your folding skills. You can use brightly colored construction paper, printer paper or origami paper if you have it. You can even draw beautiful patterns on the wings if you want.

THE EASIEST WAY TO KEEP AN ACTIVITY LOW-MESS is to only use a few craft supplies. All you need for this one is a pipe cleaner, a square of paper and scissors. You don't even need glue! Don't you just love crafts that only need three things!? There are barely any scraps and there's almost nothing to put away!

MATERIALS
- 1 square piece of paper (approximately 8½ x 8½" [21.6 x 21.6 cm])
- 1 pipe cleaner

TOOLS
- Scissors

STEP 1: Fold the square piece of paper in half into a rectangle. Open the paper up and cut along the fold to make 2 equal rectangle pieces.

STEP 2: Take one of the rectangle pieces and fold it in half to make a long, narrow rectangle. Open it up again. Take each of the corners of the rectangle and fold them inwards towards the center fold.

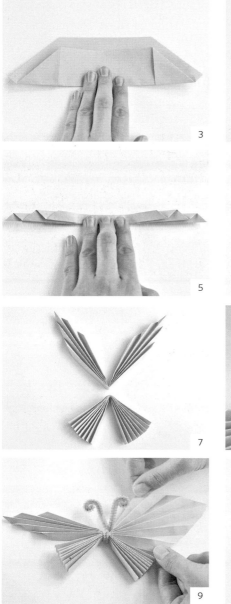

STEP 3: Turn it upside down so the folds are on the bottom. Bring the bottom of the paper upwards and fold it approximately ½ inch (1.3 cm) from the center fold.

STEP 4: Bring the top of the paper downwards, so the fold is even with the center. Continue folding the paper evenly, back and forth in opposite directions, until you reach the end.

STEP 5: Turn the paper over. Fold the top down, approximately ½ inch (1.3 cm) from the center fold. Repeat the steps, folding it evenly, back and forth in opposite directions, until you reach the end.

STEP 6: Take the other paper rectangle and fold the short edge inwards by about ½ inch (1.3 cm). Continue to fold the paper evenly, back and forth in opposite directions, until you reach the end.

STEP 7: Fold both of the folded pieces of paper in half, pinching the folds. Set out the 2 pieces so the folded points are touching each other with the paper folds fanning outwards.

STEP 8: Wrap a pipe cleaner tightly around the center, twisting to hold it together. Trim the pipe cleaners shorter, then curl the pipe cleaner ends into a spiral to make the antennae.

STEP 9: Gently pull apart the folds in each section of the paper to shape the butterfly wings.

STEP 10: Your folded paper butterfly is complete!

Painted Rock Toadstools

LEVEL OF DIFFICULTY 1/5 ✦ PARENTAL SUPERVISION
ASK A GROWN UP TO HELP WITH THE GLUE GUN.

MATERIALS
- "Multi-surface" acrylic paint (red and white)
- Disposable dinner plate
- 2 smooth rocks (1 medium and 1 small)

TOOLS
- 2 paint brushes (1 with a medium tip and 1 with a small tip)
- Low-temperature glue gun

DO YOU KNOW THE BEST WAY to keep the mess from painting projects under control? Make sure the objects that you're painting are small! Less paint = less mess.

ITS ALSO IMPORTANT to have a plan for keeping the paint contained. I love painting things in a large disposable dinner plate or on an aluminum foil lined baking sheet. You can let the rocks dry right on the plate and when you're done, just toss the plate (or aluminum foil) in the trash and the mess is gone! Don't forget to protect the table with an inexpensive plastic tablecloth, just in case.

STEP 1: Squeeze a small glob of each paint onto the disposable dinner plate. Paint the larger rock red and the smaller rock white using the paint brush with a medium tip. Allow the rocks to dry, then paint them again with a second coat of paint.

STEP 2: Keep adding coats of paint and letting them dry on the dinner plate until you are happy with the color. I added 3 coats of paint on mine.

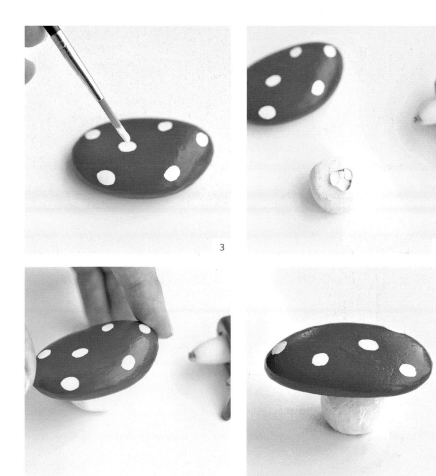

STEP 3: Using the paint brush with a small tip, paint white dots on the top of the red rock.

STEP 4: Add a generous glob of hot glue onto the white rock.

STEP 5: Press the red rock on top of the glue and hold it in place for about 30 seconds, or until the glue dries.

STEP 6: Your painted rock toadstools are complete!

HINT: Make sure you use "multi-surface" acrylic paint on the rocks (you can find it at the craft store). If your larger rock is a very dark color, paint it white before you paint it red.

3

4

5

6

Chapter 2

Under THE SEA

Explore the depths of the ocean with some of your favorite sea creatures! Whip up a family of colorful octopuses (page 34) and their long tentacle jellyfish friends (page 46) in this chapter. You might even run into some friendly mermaids. Just be sure to watch out for the shark!

⋙ LOW-MESS TIP: AVOID MESSY MATERIALS ⋘

The easiest way to keep your crafts low-mess is to avoid messy materials. Whenever you can use colored paper to make paper rolls instead of painting toilet paper rolls (like the Paper Roll Octopus [page 34] in this chapter) or whenever you can use bright and colorful materials that are already the color you need (like the Plastic Cup Whale in this chapter [page 44]), you get to leave the paint—and all the accessories and clean up that goes along with it—in the cupboard.

It's not always possible to avoid messy materials, and that's completely okay too! I'll give you a few tips to keep your painting projects under control later in this chapter and throughout the book to help you keep them as low-mess as possible.

Paper Roll Octopus (page 34), Clothespin Shark (page 36), Plastic Spoon Mermaid (page 38), Folded Ribbon Fish (page 40), Coral Reef with DIY Crystals (page 42), Plastic Cup Whale (page 44), Cupcake Liner Jellyfish (page 46), Painted Rock Sea Turtle (page 48)

Paper Roll Octopus

LEVEL OF DIFFICULTY 2/5 + PARENTAL SUPERVISION NOT REQUIRED

INSTEAD OF PAINTING TOILET PAPER ROLLS make your own rolls out of paper! It's super simple and very low-mess. These little creatures are mega cute and so easy to make.

CHOOSE YOUR FAVORITE PAPER COLORS TO MAKE YOURS. You can use printer paper, construction paper or thick paper—whatever you have at home. Then draw a happy and simple face to bring your octopus to life.

MATERIALS
- 1 piece of colored paper (any color)
- 2 medium googly eyes

TOOLS
- Scissors
- Glue stick (or something tube shaped)
- Crafter's tape
- Washable markers
- Pencil

STEP 1: Cut a piece of colored paper into a rectangle, about 6½ inches (16.5 cm) long by 5½ inches (14 cm) wide. Wrap the paper around a glue stick to shape it into a tube.

STEP 2: Add 2 rows of crafter's tape on the inside edge.

1

2

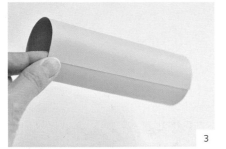

3

4

5

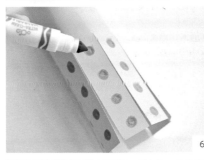

6

7

8

9

10

STEP 3: Shape it back into a tube and press along the edge where the tape is to hold it in place.

STEP 4: Use scissors to make a 3 inch (7.5 cm) long cut into one end of the tube. Next, make a 3-inch (7.5-cm) long cut right across from the first cut. Then make 2 more cuts, evenly spaced between the first 2 cuts.

STEP 5: Make 4 more cuts, evenly spaced between the first 4 cuts, to make 8 even strips at the bottom of the tube. These will be the legs.

STEP 6: Using a washable marker, color 4 evenly spaced circles on each one of the strips at the bottom of the tube.

STEP 7: Draw a smile on the front of the tube using a red washable marker.

STEP 8: Apply crafter's tape to the back of the googly eyes, then press them onto the tube above the smile. Draw 3 thin eyelashes out from each googly eye.

STEP 9: Curl each strip at the bottom of the tube around a pencil. If the curls are too tight, gently pull them out until you are happy with the shape.

STEP 10: Your paper roll octopus is complete!

Clothespin Shark

LEVEL OF DIFFICULTY 2/5 + PARENTAL SUPERVISION NOT REQUIRED.

WATCH OUT! Here comes a shark! This shark is so much fun. Pinch the clothespin and the shark mouth opens wide! Chomp—is your shark going to catch the fish? My kids loved this shark craft. They thought it was hilarious when they saw that the mouth opens up with a little fishy inside!

CRAFTER'S TAPE IS AN AWESOME CRAFT SUPPLY to keep on hand for your low-mess crafts. It doesn't drip like white glue and its sticking power is so much stronger than a glue stick. Can you think of any other animals you can make with a clothespin? Maybe a frog eating a fly? Or a dog eating a bone? It's easy to make similar crafts using the same method.

MATERIALS
- 1 piece of paper (gray)
- 2 scraps of paper (white and orange)
- 1 clothespin

TOOLS
- Pencil
- Scissors
- Glue stick
- Washable marker (black)
- Crafter's tape

STEP 1: Fold up one end of the gray paper by about 2 inches (5 cm). Draw the top half of a shark shape along the fold, making it about 6 inches (15 cm) long.

STEP 2: Cut out the shark shape and open the fold.

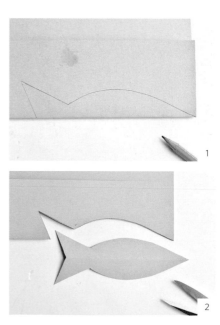

STEP 3: Cut the shark shape in half along the fold. Cut 2 more triangles from the gray paper for the top and bottom fins of the shark.

STEP 4: Cut a rectangle from the white paper, about 4 inches (10 cm) long and ½ inch (1.3 cm) wide. Cut zigzag lines across the middle of the rectangle to make the shark's teeth.

STEP 5: Use a glue stick to attach the teeth to the gray shark pieces. Trim the white paper if needed.

STEP 6: Cut out a fishy shape from a scrap of orange paper. Then cut out a small, thin rectangle, about ¾ inch (1.9 cm) long and ⅛ inch (0.3 cm) wide.

STEP 7: Use a glue stick to attach the top and bottom fins to the back of the shark pieces. Then glue the fishy shape to the thin gray rectangle and attach the rectangle to the back side of the teeth on the bottom shark piece.

STEP 8: Flip over the shark pieces to the front side. Use a black washable marker to draw an eye and some gills.

STEP 9: Carefully add a line of crafter's tape to the top and bottom of one side of the clothespin. Be careful not to overlap the glue strips or the clothespin won't open. Line up the top and bottom shark pieces and carefully press them onto the crafter's tape on the clothespin.

STEP 10: Your clothespin shark is complete!

Plastic Spoon Mermaid

LEVEL OF DIFFICULTY 3/5 ✦ PARENTAL SUPERVISION NOT REQUIRED.

MATERIALS
- Plastic spoon
- 4 pipe cleaners (1 light brown, 2 dark brown, 1 blue)
- 2 small googly eyes
- Sparkly self-adhesive craft foam (green)

TOOLS
- Washable markers (red and black)
- Crafter's tape
- Scissors

ITS AMAZING WHAT YOU CAN CREATE from every day objects. Even when they have nothing to do with crafts! Did you ever imagine that a plastic spoon would also make the perfect mermaid? What else do you think you could make from a plastic spoon?

YOU'LL NEED A BIT OF CRAFTER'S TAPE to attach the hair, but there's no glue needed for this one. You're going to be wrapping the pipe cleaners around the spoon and using self-adhesive craft foam. Simple and clean!

STEP 1: Press the googly eyes onto the crafter's tape. Carefully peel them off, making sure the tape sticks to the back of the eyes. Press the eyes into position on the inside of the spoon.

Draw a smile and freckles onto the inside of the spoon using the black and red washable markers. If you aren't happy with the face you drew, wipe it off with a damp paper towel and try again!

STEP 2: Fold the light brown pipe cleaner in half to find the middle. Open it back up and place the middle of the pipe cleaner behind the plastic spoon. Wind each side of the pipe cleaner tightly around the spoon, one time each.

Bring the ends of the pipe cleaner back to the middle of the spoon. Bend a small piece forward on both ends to make the mermaid's hands. Then make a bend in the middle of each arm to make the elbows.

STEP 3: Starting at the neck of the spoon, wind the blue pipe cleaner around and down the spoon, looping over the arms twice to hold them in place. Continue winding downwards around the spoon until you run out of pipe cleaner.

STEP 4: Apply several rows of crafter's tape at an angle at the back of the spoon near the tip.

STEP 5: Wind one of the dark brown pipe cleaners around the head at an angle, pressing it onto the crafter's tape as you go to make sure it stays in place. Use scissors to trim any extra pipe cleaner.

STEP 6: Cut the second dark brown pipe cleaner in half. Be sure to fold the pipe cleaner in half to find the middle first. Then, bend and shape the two pipe cleaner halves into a hair style for the mermaid, using the spoon as a guide for the head shape.

STEP 7: Apply crafter's tape around the edge of the spoon and carefully attach the mermaid's hair. Add more tape if you need to and shape the hair as you go.

STEP 8: Using the self-adhesive sparkly green craft foam, cut out a rectangular shape that's the same width as the plastic spoon and about 3 inches (7.8 cm) long. Cut another piece of foam in the shape of a mermaid tail.

STEP 9: Remove the self-adhesive backing from the craft foam rectangle and press it onto the spoon, starting right below the pipe cleaner waist. Trim off any extra craft foam at the bottom of the spoon. Add a small line of crafter's tape to the back of the mermaid tail and press it onto the bottom of the spoon, right on top of the rectangular piece of sparkly craft foam.

STEP 10: Your plastic spoon mermaid is complete!

Folded Ribbon Fish

LEVEL OF DIFFICULTY 5/5 + PARENTAL SUPERVISION NOT REQUIRED.

DON'T LIMIT YOUR FOLDING SKILLS TO PAPER. Try folding with ribbons too! Ribbons give an awesome soft texture and are often forgotten when you're thinking of craft supplies. You don't need a needle and thread, or even glue—just use crafter's tape. Crafter's tape is my favorite low-mess craft supply!

I MADE THESE LITTLE RIBBON FISH just to play with, but wouldn't they make awesome hair clips? Attach them to a plastic hair clip with glue from the glue gun. Or you can make them into pins, key chains or even necklaces. What will you do with yours?

MATERIALS
- Thick (⅝" [1.6-cm] wide) ribbon
- Thin (⅜" [1-cm] wide) ribbon
- 1 small googly eye

TOOLS
- Scissors
- Small ruler
- Crafter's tape

STEP 1: Cut 2 pieces of the thin ribbon, one 2½ inches (6.5 cm) and one 3½ inches (9 cm) long. Cut one piece of the thick ribbon, 6 inches (15 cm) long.

STEP 2: Cross one end of the thick ribbon over the other to create a fish shape, leaving a small opening at the midpoint for the mouth. Add a strip of crafter's tape where the ribbon crosses itself and pinch it to hold the ribbon in place.

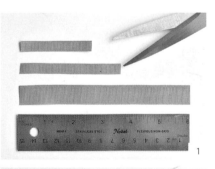

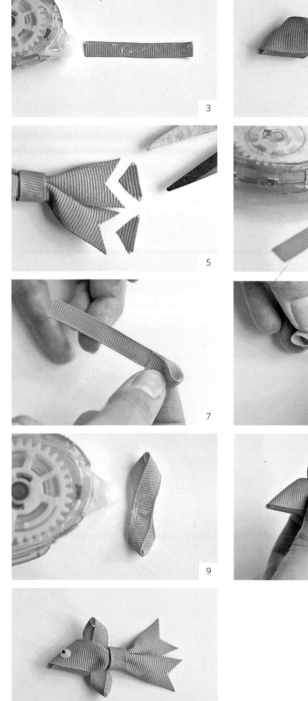

STEP 3: Add a strip of crafter's tape along one side of the 2½-inch (6.5-cm) piece of thin ribbon.

STEP 4: Wrap the 2½-inch (6.5-cm) long piece of thin ribbon around the midpoint of the fish shape to make the body. Pinch it tightly so the crafter's tape holds it in place.

STEP 5: Cut a triangle shape out from the ends of the thick ribbon to make a tail shape.

STEP 6: Add a ½-inch (1.3-cm) strip of crafter's tape in the middle of the 3.5-inch (9-cm) piece of thin ribbon.

STEP 7: Take one end of the thin ribbon and twist it over and around to make a loop and press it to the crafter's tape in the middle.

STEP 8: Take the other end and twist it over and around to make another loop and press it to the crafter's tape in the middle so the 2 ends meet.

STEP 9: Add a ½-inch (1.3-cm) strip of crafter's tape in the middle of the twisted ribbon piece, on the side where the 2 ends meet.

STEP 10: Position the twisted ribbon piece behind the fish's head, just beside the body and pinch tightly to hold it in place. Add crafter's tape to the back of the googly eye and press it into position on the fish's head.

STEP 11: Your folded ribbon fish is complete!

Coral Reef with ✦ DIY Crystals ✦

LEVEL OF DIFFICULTY 3/5 ✦ PARENTAL SUPERVISION
ASK A GROWN UP TO HELP WITH THE BORAX MIXTURE.

MATERIALS
- 4 pipe cleaners
- Craft stick
- String
- ½ cup (120 ml) borax (available at the supermarket in the laundry section)
- 2 cups (475 ml) boiling water
- 2-cup (475-ml) mason jar

TOOLS
- Scissors

THIS CRAFT DOUBLES AS A SCIENCE EXPERIMENT! When you leave the solution overnight, cube-shaped crystals grow on the pipe cleaners, almost like magic. But don't worry—if you don't have any borax, or if you don't want to wait overnight, you can easily stop when you've made your pipe cleaner reef. Now that's a simple and clean project!

AND SPEAKING OF CLEAN, after you've grown your crystals, you can pour the borax mixture into a load of dirty laundry—it's a laundry booster after all! Did you ever think you'd have a craft that also makes your laundry cleaner?!

STEP 1: Fold one of the pipe cleaners in half to make a "V" shape. Fold one side of the V in half again, twisting the end around itself to keep it in place. Fold the other end of the pipe cleaner down a bit more than half way so it's longer than the other side. Twist the end around itself to keep it in place. You should have an uneven "V" shape.

STEP 2: Cut 2 of the pipe cleaners into 4 or 5 pieces each, all different lengths. You'll need 8 to 10 pieces total.

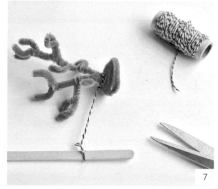

STEP 3: Twist a short pipe cleaner piece around the pipe cleaner "V" shape.

STEP 4: Keep adding pipe cleaner pieces to the "V" shape by twisting the end of the short pipe cleaner pieces around the "V" shape. Add them near the tip, middle and down near the fold on both sides of the "V" until you're happy with the coral shape.

STEP 5: Take the last pipe cleaner and wind it around the bottom of the "V" shape to make an even spiral base for the coral to stand on.

STEP 6: Bend each of the pipe cleaner tips on the coral upwards and adjust the shape until you're happy with it.

Feel free to stop here if you don't want to make the crystals today. Your pipe cleaner coral piece looks great just like this!

STEP 7: Cut a piece of string, about 6 inches (15.3 cm) long. Tie one end of the string around the base of the coral. Tie the other end of the string around a craft stick, leaving about 1 inch (2.5 cm) between the base of the coral and the craft stick.

STEP 8: Add ½ cup (120 ml) of borax to 2 cups (475 ml) of boiling water. Stir until the borax is dissolved and the mixture becomes clear. If the mixture looks cloudy, microwave it for 1 minute to help dissolve the borax.

Lower the pipe cleaner coral piece into a mason jar, resting the craft stick on the top of the jar. Make sure the coral isn't touching the bottom or sides of the jar. Adjust the length of the string if you need to and trim off any extra string. Carefully pour the hot borax mixture into the jar, filling it until the coral piece is completely covered.

STEP 9: Let the jar sit untouched for 6 to 24 hours. The crystals will grow on the pipe cleaner as the mixture cools. Lift the pipe cleaner and carefully remove it from the jar. Use a fork to loosen it from the sides and bottom of the jar if it's stuck.

Lay the coral piece on a paper towel and use scissors to cut the string off the base of the coral. Let the coral piece dry for 2 to 3 hours.

STEP 10: Your coral reef with do-it-yourself crystals is complete!

Plastic Cup Whale

LEVEL OF DIFFICULTY 1/5 ⚬ PARENTAL SUPERVISION
ASK A GROWN UP TO HELP CUT THE X IN THE TOP OF THE PLASTIC CUP.

WHATS THE EASIEST WAY to make a craft low-mess? Find craft materials that are the color you need!

FORGET ABOUT PAINTING a foam or paper cup (although that's definitely an option if you're in a pinch!). Blue plastic cups are readily available—even the grocery store has them sometimes—and blue is perfect for whales. This plastic cup whale is super simple to make and great for all ages.

MATERIALS
- 1 blue plastic cup
- 1 piece of thick paper (blue)
- 3 pipe cleaners (2 white and 1 black)
- 2 large googly eyes

TOOLS
- Scissors
- Pencil
- Crafter's tape

STEP 1: Using the point of the scissors, cut a small X shape into the middle of the top of the cup.

STEP 2: Draw 2 large tear drop shapes (about 3 inches [7.5 cm] long) and a tail shape (about 4 inches [10 cm] long) from the thick blue paper. Cut out each of the pieces.

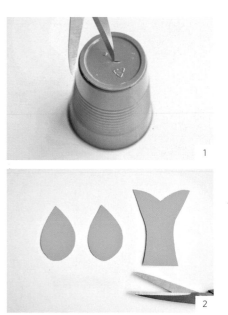

STEP 3: Cut a piece of black pipe cleaner, about 2½ inches (6.4 cm) long. Bend it into a smile shape.

STEP 4: Take each of the white pipe cleaners and bend them in half to make a "V" shape. Curl each of the pipe cleaner ends into a small spiral.

STEP 5: Gently poke the points of the white pipe cleaners (the bottom of the "V" shapes) into the hole at the top of the plastic cup. On the inside of the cup, bend each of the pipe cleaner ends towards the underside of the cup to hold them in place.

STEP 6: Add crafter's tape to the back of the googly eyes and pipe-cleaner smile and position them on the plastic cup to make the whale's face.

STEP 7: Gently bend the tail so that it curls upwards. Make a fold at the straight end of the tail, about ½-inch (1.3-cm) wide.

STEP 8: Add a strip of crafter's tape to the inside of the fold on the tail and attach it to the inside of the blue cup.

STEP 9: Add a couple rows of crafter's tape to the rounded end of the tear drops and gently press one to each side of the plastic cup with the points going towards the back of the whale.

STEP 10: Your plastic cup whale is complete!

Cupcake Liner Jelly Fish

LEVEL OF DIFFICULTY 1/5 ⊕ PARENTAL SUPERVISION NOT REQUIRED.

MATERIALS
- Gift wrapping ribbon
- 2 cupcake liners
- 2 large googly eyes

TOOLS
- Scissors
- Tape
- Crafter's tape

RUNNING LOW ON CRAFT SUPPLIES? Check out your kitchen and gift wrapping stash instead. Cupcake liners and gift wrapping ribbons are awesome for crafts! And that's exactly what we used to make these cupcake liner jelly fish. And with no leftover scraps at the end, the clean up for this one is easy!

GIFT WRAPPING RIBBON normally has a natural curl to it, so when you tape it to the cupcake liner, it makes wonderful jellyfish tentacles. When you fly them through the air the ribbons bob up and down, curling and un-curling. It looks like it's floating, just like a real jellyfish.

STEP 1: Cut 12 pieces of gift wrapping ribbon, about 18 inches (46 cm) long each.

STEP 2: Attach one end of each piece of ribbon to the top of one of the cupcake liners using tape. Keep adding ribbon pieces, going around in a circle until all the pieces are used up.

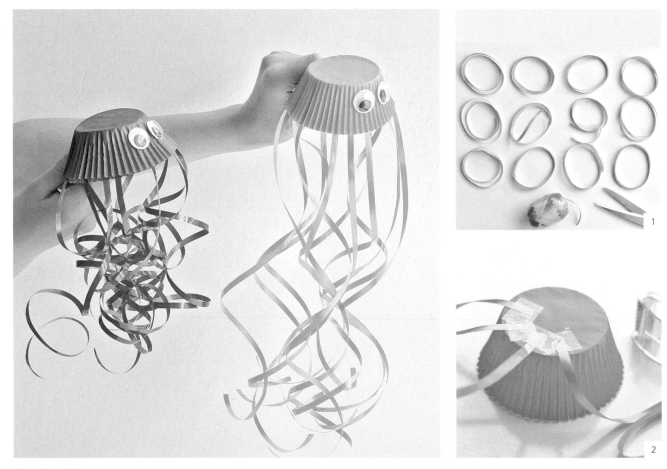

3

4

5

6

STEP 3: Add a few strips of crafters tape to the top of the cupcake liner, over the ribbon and tape pieces.

STEP 4: Slide the second cupcake liner over the top of the first cupcake liner.

STEP 5: Make sure the cupcake liners are lined up evenly, then pinch the 2 liners together. Add crafter's tape to the back of the googly eyes and gently press them onto the cupcake liner.

STEP 6: Your cupcake liner jelly fish is complete!

Painted Rock Sea Turtle

LEVEL OF DIFFICULTY 1/5 ◆ PARENTAL SUPERVISION NOT REQUIRED.

MATERIALS
- 1 smooth rock
- Liquid chalk markers
- 1 scrap of green paper
- 1 medium pom pom (green)
- 2 googly eyes

TOOLS
- Scissors
- Crafter's tape

HAVE YOU EVER COME ACROSS the perfect rock when you're out on a nature walk? My daughters are always bringing home special rocks, but we never know what to do with them. These painted rock sea turtles are the perfect solution. What better idea than to use them for crafting!

YOU CAN FIND LIQUID CHALK MARKERS at the craft store or business supply store. They're meant for drawing on glass, but they're also a perfect addition to your collection of craft supplies. Coloring with a chalk marker is less messy than using paint, and it dries much faster.

STEP 1: Color 3 circles down the middle of the rock with the chalk markers. Color 4 more circles, centered on either side of the middle circles. Allow the liquid chalk to dry for about 5 to 10 minutes each time you add a new color.

STEP 2: Choose a different color and fill in the area between the circles, allowing the liquid chalk to dry. Then with another color, add a border around the painted area and allow the border to dry.

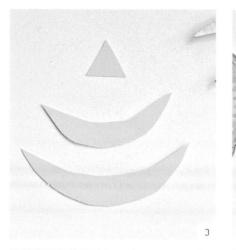

STEP 3: Cut out one large and one medium crescent shape from the green paper. Cut a small triangle for the tail.

STEP 4: Use crafter's tape to attach the paper legs and tail to the bottom of the rock.

STEP 5: Attach the googly eyes to the green pom pom using crafter's tape, then attach the pom pom to the front of the rock.

STEP 6: Your painted rock sea turtle is complete!

Chapter 3

Summer at THE BEACH

Is there anything more fun than a day at the beach!? Make yourself a new beach bag (page 60) and umbrella (page 56) and chill out under the sun with the beaded pipe-cleaner beach friends (page 54) you just made. If there's time, they can take a trip on your smart little cork sailboat or catch some waves on your new surfboard.

⩓ LOW-MESS TIP: ORGANIZE YOUR CRAFT SUPPLIES ⩔

We're going to use all sorts of fun craft supplies in this chapter like corks, washi tape, glass beads and even sea shells! It's really important to have somewhere to put all of your leftover supplies. One of the secrets to keeping your crafts tidy is making sure your craft supplies are just a little bit organized. It's not hard, I promise!

I recommend using 2 boxes. You'll need a large box to hold all of your craft materials (those are the things your crafts are made from, like pipe cleaners, pom poms, googly eyes, craft foam, etc.) and a smaller box to hold all of your craft tools (those are the things that cut, stick and write on your crafts, like scissors, glue, tape, markers, etc.). If you do your best to keep things organized it goes a long way to help you stay tidy while you're crafting.

Cork Sail Boat

LEVEL OF DIFFICULTY 2/5 ♦ PARENTAL SUPERVISION NOT REQUIRED.

THESE BOATS ACTUALLY FLOAT IN WATER! Take them out for a sail in a baking dish full of water, or even into the bathtub. Blow on the back of the sails and watch them go. They don't sit still for very long!

DON'T FORGET ABOUT ELASTICS when you're making your low-mess crafts. The elastic does all the work so there's no need for glue, or any adhesive for that matter! They're a simple way to hold your boat together with zero mess.

MATERIALS

- Sparkly craft foam
- 1 wooden skewer
- Red electrical tape
- 3 wine corks
- 1 "L"-shaped hook with a screw end (or a regular screw and a screw driver)
- 2 wide elastics (the elastics that hold broccoli together are perfect!)

TOOLS

- Scissors

STEP 1: Cut a trapezoid or rectangle shape from the craft foam, about 4 inches (10 cm) wide by 3½ inches (9 cm) tall.

STEP 2: Gently pinch the top and bottom of the trapezoid shape inwards to give the sail a bit of a curve shape.

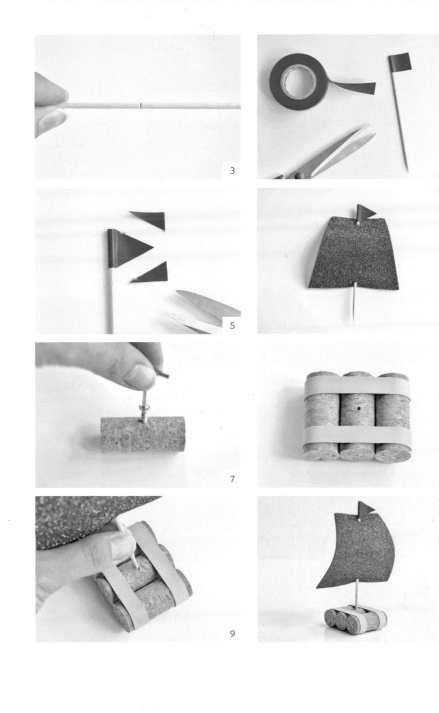

STEP 3: Use scissors to trim the wooden skewer to about 5 inches (12.5 cm) long. If your scissors won't cut through the skewer, use them to make a deep indent all the way around the skewer, then snap the skewer at the indent.

STEP 4: Cut a piece of red electrical tape about 2 inches (5 cm) long. Place the flat end of the wooden skewer in the middle of the tape and wrap it around the skewer to make a flag, making sure the ends of the tape line up evenly.

STEP 5: Cut the corners off the rectangle to make a triangular flag.

STEP 6: Carefully poke the pointy end of the wooden skewer through the center of the top and bottom of the craft foam sail, about ½ inch (1.3 cm) from each edge.

STEP 7: Use the screw end of the "L"-shaped hook to make a hole in the middle of one of the corks.

STEP 8: Line up 3 corks side by side (make sure the one with the hole is in the middle), and stretch 2 wide elastics over the corks to hold them together.

STEP 9: Push the pointy end of the wooden skewer into the hole in the middle cork.

STEP 10: Your cork sail boat is complete!

> **HINT:** Wine corks aren't as common as they used to be, so if you don't have any wine-drinking family members you can get corks from, you can also get bags of wine corks at the craft store.

Beaded Pipe Cleaner People

LEVEL OF DIFFICULTY 5/5 ✦ PARENTAL SUPERVISION NOT REQUIRED.

THESE FRIENDLY BEACH PEOPLE have elbow and knee joints, so you can bend them however you like! They can sit cross-legged, lie down on their beach towel or wave to their friends. You can personalize them so easily. Choose the colors, be creative with their clothes and don't forget to style the hair.

I LOVE USING MATERIALS that fold and twist to keep things together. Add the beads and straw pieces then bend the pipe cleaners to hold them in place. That's it! The pipe cleaners are going to do all the work here, so there's no glue required.

MATERIALS
- 2 drinking straws
- 2 pipe cleaners
- 9 pony beads
- 1 wooden bead (about ¾" [1.9 cm])

TOOLS
- Scissors
- 1 gel pen (black)

STEP 1: Cut the straws into 8 pieces. You'll need 4 pieces, about ½ inch (1.3 cm) long each and another 4 pieces, about 1 inch (2.5 cm) long each. The short pieces are used on the arms and the long pieces are used on the legs. Use different colored straws to make different clothing pieces.

STEP 2: Line up 2 pipe cleaners side by side and slide 4 pony beads onto the pipe cleaners, until they are about ⅓ of the way from the end.

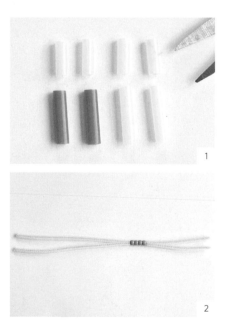

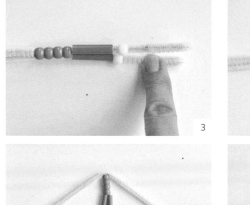

3

STEP 3: On the shorter end of the pipe cleaners, slide a 1-inch (2.5 cm) long straw piece onto each of the 2 pipe cleaner ends. Slide a pony bead onto each of the pipe cleaner ends.

Fold in the 2 ends of the pipe cleaners by about 1 inch (2.5 cm).

4

STEP 4: Slide another 1-inch (2.5 cm) straw piece over each of the 2 pipe cleaner ends. Bend the 2 pipe cleaner ends sticking out from the straws upwards to make the feet.

STEP 5: Rotate the doll so that the feet are at the bottom. Bend the 2 pipe cleaner pieces at the top downwards to make two really long arms.

5

6

STEP 6: Bend the 2 pipe cleaner ends upwards again into a "W" shape, so that the arms are just long enough to go to the bead used as the knee joint. Then cross the 2 ends of the pipe cleaner into an "X" shape, so that they overlap at the top of the pony beads.

STEP 7: Slide one of the ½-inch (1.3-cm) straw pieces onto each arm (the arms are the bottom 2 pieces of the "X" shape).

7

8

STEP 8: Slide a bead onto each of the arms for the elbow joint. Then slide another ½-inch (1.3-cm) straw piece below each of the elbow beads.

Bend the pipe cleaner ends sticking out from the straws upwards, tightly against the straws, to make the hands.

STEP 9: Bring the top 2 pipe cleaner ends together and slide on the last pony bead, pushing it tightly against the top of the arms. This will be the neck.

9

10

STEP 10: Use the gel pen to draw a happy little face onto the wooden bead.

STEP 11: Slide the wooden bead onto the pipe cleaners so that it covers the pony bead used as the neck.

Bend the 2 pipe cleaner ends back into the top of the wooden bead, as if you were making bunny ears. Then bend the 2 "bunny ears" downwards to shape the hair.

11

12

STEP 12: Your beaded pipe cleaner person is complete!

Tissue Paper Beach
≋ Umbrella ≋

LEVEL OF DIFFICULTY 4/5 ✦ PARENTAL SUPERVISION
ASK A GROWN UP TO HELP WITH THE GLUE GUN.

MATERIALS
- 1 piece of construction paper
- Small round bowl or plate (about 4.5" [11.5 cm] across)
- 1 piece of tissue paper
- 1 wooden skewer
- 1 small plastic bead

TOOLS
- Pencil
- Scissors
- Glue stick
- Low-temperature glue gun

IS THERE ANYTHING MORE RELAXING than sitting under the shade of a big beach umbrella on the warm and soft sand? This little beach umbrella reminds me of those straw huts you see at the beach. Except you can make yours any color you like. You can even use these umbrellas to make your own fancy beach drinks!

GLUE STICKS ARE A GREAT LOW-MESS CRAFT TOOL to keep in your craft stash. They don't drip and the glue dries almost instantly. Remember to apply the glue stick to small areas at a time as you press on the tissue paper fringe. A little bit of planning and patience goes a long way to keeping you out of a sticky situation!

STEP 1: On the construction paper, trace around the edge of the bowl and cut out the circle shape. Fold the circle shape in half then open it up again.

STEP 2: Fold the circle shape in half again, so when you open it up the folds make an even "X" with 4 equal quarters. Fold the circle in half 2 more times until you have 4 folds dividing the circle into 8 equal triangle sections.

3

4

5

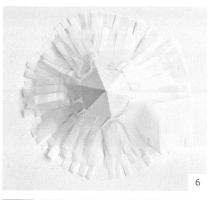

6

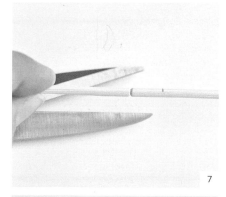

7

8

9

10

STEP 3: Cut one of the triangles out from the cirlce, as if you were cutting out one piece of pie. Use a glue stick to apply glue to the triangle section right beside the piece that was cut out.

STEP 4: Take the edge of the other side of the cut out piece and overlap it onto the glue, so that the edge lines up with the fold. Press it onto the glue and you should end up with an umbrella shape.

STEP 5: Cut out 3 long strips of tissue paper, about 2 inches (5 cm) wide. Make 1½ inch (3.8 cm) long cuts into the strip of tissue paper, spaced very close together along the entire length to create a fringe. To speed up the process, fold the strip of tissue paper in half several times before you cut, until it's only about 3 inches (7.5 cm) long. Then make the fringe cuts through the folded piece before you open it up again.

STEP 6: Using a glue stick, apply glue along the entire bottom edge of the construction paper umbrella shape. Take one end of the tissue paper fringe and press it onto the glue, wrapping it around the circle shape and pressing it to the construction paper as you go until you've gone around the entire bottom edge.

Overlap the layers and continue gluing on the tissue paper fringe, wrapping it around the umbrella until you've reached the top point. Trim off any extra tissue paper.

STEP 7: Use scissors to trim the wooden skewer to about 5 inches (12.5 cm) long. If your scissors won't cut through the skewer, use them to make a deep indent all the way around the skewer, then snap the skewer at the indent.

STEP 8: Add a generous glob of glue from the glue gun into the point of the umbrella on the underside. Push the pointy end of the wooden skewer into the glue so it just pokes through the top of the umbrella. Hold the skewer in place for at least 30 seconds until the hot glue dries.

STEP 9: Add a small dot of hot glue to the outside point of the umbrella and attach the small bead.

STEP 10: Your tissue paper beach umbrella is complete!

✦ Glass Bead ✦
Crabs

LEVEL OF DIFFICULTY 3/5 ✦ PARENTAL SUPERVISION
ASK A GROWN UP TO HELP WITH THE GLUE GUN.

GLASS BEADS ARE ALSO CALLED "VASE FILLER" and can be found in the decorating section at the dollar store or craft store. They are small, shiny and super fun to use in crafts!

THESE CRABS ARE SUCH A FUN LITTLE PROJECT. You only need a few things to make them and there's barely any scraps to clean up! You can see the color through the glass bead and the little crab legs look they are ready to scurry off into the sand. What color will your crabs be?

STEP 1: Place the glass bead onto a scrap of red paper and trace around the shape with a pencil.

STEP 2: Cut out the small paper shape and attach it to the bottom of the glass bead using a small glob of hot glue from the glue gun. You'll be able to see the glue through the glass bead, so make sure you add enough glue so that it spreads out evenly across the entire bottom.

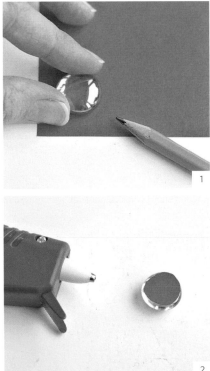

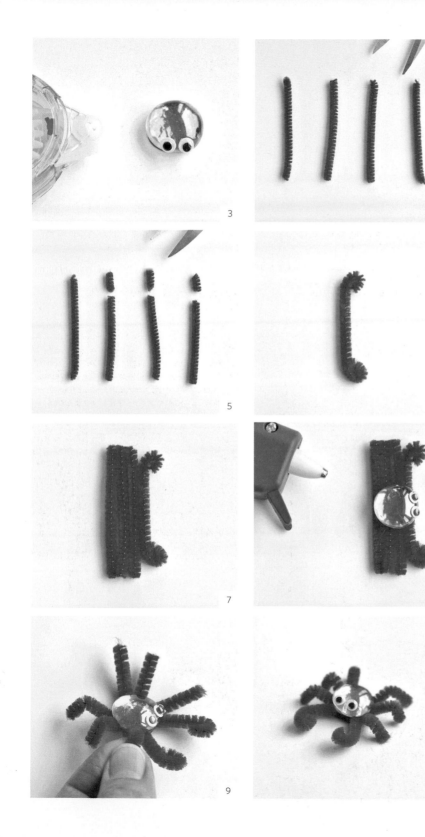

STEP 3: Turn the glass bead over and attach the googly eyes to the top of the glass bead using crafter's tape.

STEP 4: Cut the pipe cleaner into 4 equal pieces. (Fold the pipe cleaner in half to find the center then cut it at the fold. Then fold each of those pieces in half to find the center, and cut them at the fold).

STEP 5: Trim off about ¼ inch (0.6 cm) from the end of 3 of the pipe cleaners.

STEP 6: Take each end of the longest pipe cleaner piece and bend them in towards the middle to make a claw shape.

STEP 7: Line up all 4 of the pipe cleaner pieces side by side, so that the piece with the claws is at the front.

STEP 8: Add hot glue to the bottom of the glass bead, then carefully press it onto the middle of the pipe cleaner pieces.

STEP 9: Bend each of the pipe cleaner pieces outwards to spread them into crab legs. Bend the pipe cleaner tips downwards to give the legs some shape.

STEP 10: Your glass bead crab is complete!

♡ Washi Tape ♡ Beach Bag

LEVEL OF DIFFICULTY 2/5 ✦ PARENTAL SUPERVISION NOT REQUIRED.

WASHI TAPE IS A NEWER CRAFT MATERIAL (at least to me), but its potential is endless! You get all these amazing patterns without needing to color or paint a thing! Snip the tape, press it back on the roll and there's zero mess.

THESE LITTLE BEACH TOTES ARE SO SIMPLE to make, and they look so cool. My kids had lots of fun filling them with all sorts of fun little items and putting them on their doll's arms. They are the perfect size for the doll house.

MATERIALS
- Plastic craft supply zip bag (about 3 x 2" [7.5 x 5 cm])
- Washi tape
- Colored baker's twine

TOOLS
- Scissors
- Small hole punch

STEP 1: Cut off the zippered part of the bag so the remaining bag is about 2 inches (5 cm) deep.

STEP 2: Stretch a straight layer of washi tape along the bottom fold of the plastic bag, wrapping it until you have gone around the entire bag. Use scissors to make a tidy cut in the washi tape.

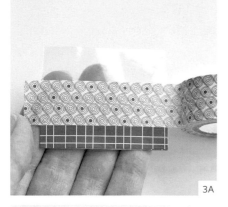

3A

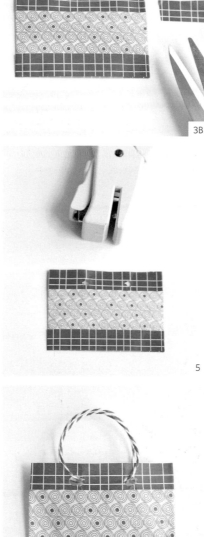

3B

STEP 3: Wrap a second and third row of washi tape around the entire plastic bag, just above the row below it, until the bag is covered with washi tape.

STEP 4: Trim off any extra plastic bag that's left above the washi tape, being careful to cut as close to the washi tape as possible.

STEP 5: Use a small hole punch to cut out 2 holes at the top of the bag (the end of the bag that opens).

STEP 6: Cut a piece of colored baker's twine to about 6½ inches (16.5 cm) long. Thread the piece of twine through the holes and tie a knot at the top. Trim off any extra twine and pull the twine so that the knot is hidden inside the bag.

STEP 7: Your washi tape beach bag is complete!

4

5

6

7

Straw Weaving Beach Towel

LEVEL OF DIFFICULTY 4/5 ✦ PARENTAL SUPERVISION NOT REQUIRED.

THIS CRAFT IS AN EXCELLENT INTRODUCTION to weaving. And you don't need any fancy tools, just drinking straws, tape, yarn, and scissors! It's so easy to clean up when you're only using 4 things! These beach towels are really quick to make. When you're done you won't believe you made it yourself!

ONCE YOU'VE MASTERED THIS METHOD of weaving, don't stop—try weaving until the piece is long enough to wrap around your wrist. Tie the ends of the yarn together and you've made a quick and simple bracelet with the exact same method!

MATERIALS
- 4 drinking straws
- Yarn (I like to use multicolored yarn, but solid colored yarn will work too.)

TOOLS
- Masking tape
- Scissors

STEP 1: Place the drinking straws together, side-by-side, and tape the ends together using masking tape.

STEP 2: Cut 4 pieces of yarn about the length of 2 drinking straws put together (about 16 inches [40.5 cm] long). Then thread each piece of yarn through one of the straws.

1

2

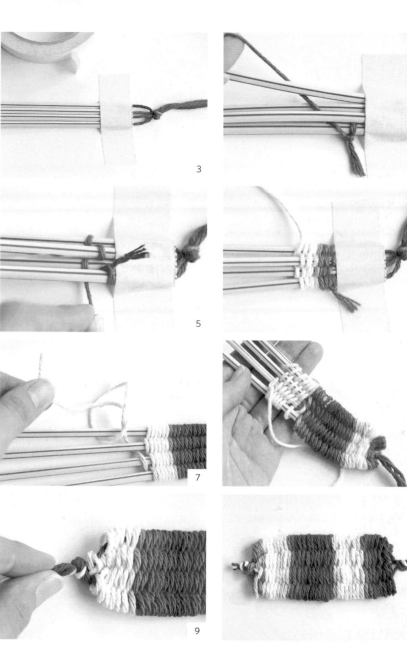

STEP 3: Tie a knot in the yarn at the end with the tape. Then tape the straws to a flat surface.

STEP 4: Tie a knot around the first straw. Then slide it under the second straw, over the third straw and under the fourth straw.

STEP 5: Pull it back towards you over the fourth straw, under the third straw, over the second straw and under the first straw. Use your fingers to push the yarn towards the tape as you go, to keep the rows close together.

STEP 6: Pull the yarn around and over the first straw and continue weaving, going under the second straw, over the third straw, under the fourth straw, and then back over the fourth straw, under the third straw, over the second straw and under the first straw.

STEP 7: Continue this weaving pattern until you're happy with the length of your beach towel. Cut the yarn, leaving about 6 inches (15 cm) at the end, then tie it around the last straw, where you finished weaving.

STEP 8: Remove the tape holding the straws together, then carefully push the yarn off the straws. Make sure the yarn in the straws doesn't slip out as you push off the woven rows.

If your woven towel looks crooked, lay it flat on the table and use your fingers to push the woven layers towards the knotted end and to shape it into a rectangle.

STEP 9: Pinch together the 4 loose yarn pieces and tie them into a knot, as close to the woven rows as possible. Trim off the extra yarn from the knots at both ends.

STEP 10: Your straw woven beach towel is complete!

Craft Foam Surfboard

LEVEL OF DIFFICULTY 1/5 ✦ PARENTAL SUPERVISION NOT REQUIRED.

MATERIALS
- 1 piece of thick paper (or a cereal box)
- 1 piece of craft foam (white)
- 1 piece of self-adhesive craft foam (any color)

TOOLS
- Pencil
- Scissors
- Washable markers
- Ruler

ARE YOU READY to take your small toys or figurines on a ride? Because these little surfboards will actually float in water with a small toy on top! Don't worry if the washable marker gets wet, just wash it off and you can draw a new brilliant pattern on your surf board next time.

I ALWAYS RECOMMEND using washable art supplies whenever possible to keep messes to a minimum. You can use permanent markers instead of washable if you don't want the pattern to wash off your surf board in the water. But be careful, because if you get permanent marker on your fingers, it will take a few days to wash off of you too!

STEP 1: Make a fold in the thick paper and draw half a surfboard shape along the fold about 5 inches (12.5 cm) long. Cut out the surfboard shape and open it up.

STEP 2: Trace the paper surfboard shape onto the white craft foam, then trace a second one onto the self-adhesive craft foam. Cut out the 2 craft foam surfboard shapes.

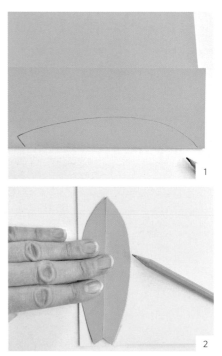

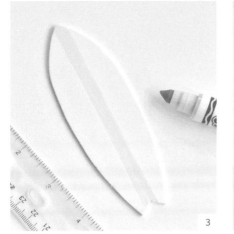

STEP 3: Draw a pattern on the top of the surfboard in pencil. Then color it in using washable markers. Try swirls, flowers, stripes, trees or waves, all in different colors.

STEP 4: Peel off the backing from the self adhesive craft foam.

STEP 5: Carefully line up the 2 foam surfboard pieces and gently press them together, being careful not to smudge your coloring.

STEP 6: Your craft foam surfboard is complete!

3

4

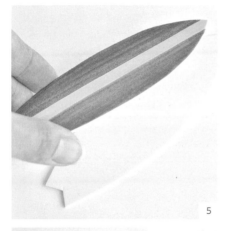

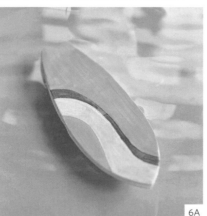

5

6A

6B

Painted Seashell Clams

LEVEL OF DIFFICULTY 1/5 ✦ PARENTAL SUPERVISION
ASK A GROWN UP TO HELP WITH THE GLUE GUN.

MATERIALS
- Acrylic paint
- Disposable dinner plate
- 2 matching seashell halves
- 2 medium googly eyes

TOOLS
- Paint brush
- Low-temperature glue gun

DO YOU EVER COLLECT SEA SHELLS at the beach? This craft is perfect for them! If you don't live anywhere near a beach, don't worry, you can also buy sea shells at the craft store or dollar store. These adorable little clams look like they're peeking out of their shells.

KEEP THE PAINTING MESS to a minimum by painting your sea shells on a large plastic plate or in an aluminum foil-covered baking sheet. Paint the shells right on top of the plate and leave them there until they are completely dry. The mess is contained and clean up is easy.

STEP 1: Squeeze a small amount of paint onto the disposable plate. Paint the outside of the seashells a bright color, or choose several bright colors for a bright seashell family.

STEP 2: Carefully set the seashells down on the plate and let them dry. Paint 2 or 3 coats until the color is strong and consistent, letting the paint dry between each coat.

3

4

STEP 3: Squeeze a generous line of hot glue from the glue gun onto the inside back part of one of the seashells.

STEP 4: Line up the second seashell over the first seashell and carefully press it into the glue, making sure you leave the front part open by about ¼ inch (0.6 cm).

STEP 5: Add a small dab of hot glue to the top and bottom of the seashell and press the googly eye into position on the hot glue. Do the same for the second googly eye.

STEP 6: Your painted seashell clams are complete!

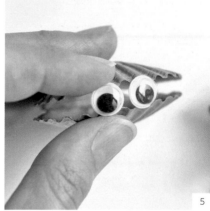

5

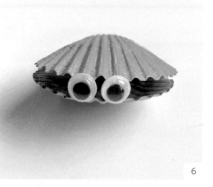

6

Chapter 4

Animals AT THE ZOO

Monkeys and lions and penguins, oh my! Which one to make first? It's easy to craft these adorable zoo animals. Save up those toilet paper rolls and get ready to start using your construction paper stash. You're going to create some awesome (and adorable) animals!

⤳ LOW-MESS TIP: USE WASHABLE ART SUPPLIES ⤳

Always try to use washable art supplies whenever you can. Choose washable markers instead of permanent markers. Use washable paint whenever possible and try to find glue that says "washable" on the label. You can even buy washable crayons and washable glitter glue.

That way, if you accidentally get marker on your hands while you're making the Paper Roll Giraffe (page 80), it will wash right off. Or if you accidentally put your elbow right on top of the glue stick you used to make the Paper Roll Lion (page 70), it won't stain your clothes. There's nothing worse than having marker that stays on your hands for days!

Paper Roll Lion (page 70), Foam Cup Zebra (page 72), Pipe Cleaner Monkey (page 74),
Pipe Cleaner Flamingo (page 76), Paper Roll Elephant (page 78), Paper Roll Giraffe (page 80),
Mini Paper Penguins (page 82), Folded Paper Peacocks (page 84)

Paper Roll
≈ Lion ≈

LEVEL OF DIFFICULTY 4/5 ✦ PARENTAL SUPERVISION NOT REQUIRED.

DON'T BOTHER PAINTING THE FOAM BALL, cover it with tissue paper instead! It's such a quick and easy way to give something color with zero mess!

WHEN YOU'RE MAKING YOUR LOW-MESS CRAFTS, always keep an eye out for materials that can stick together without any glue. When you press the pipe cleaners into the foam ball, they stick there all by themselves. It's amazing to see how quickly simple materials can be brought together to make a fun looking animal.

STEP 1: Cut out a rectangle of construction paper just large enough to cover an entire toilet paper roll. Use tape to hold one end of the construction paper to the paper roll. Then apply glue to the entire inside surface of the construction paper with a glue stick. Roll it around the toilet paper roll, pressing it to the paper roll as you go.

STEP 2: Cut out a square of tissue paper, about 10 x 10 inches (25.5 x 25.5 cm). Place the foam ball in the middle, then wrap the tissue paper tightly around the ball. Twist the ends of the tissue paper tightly.

Cut off the twisted end of the tissue paper, about ¼ inch (0.6 cm) from the ball and add some tape over the twist to hold it in place.

1

STEP 3: Cut each of the 5 pipe cleaners into 3 equal pieces. (You'll end up with 15 pieces total.)

Take 2 of the pipe cleaner pieces (try to choose longer ones) and cut off a ½-inch (1.3-cm) piece from each one. Set these 2 small pieces aside. We'll use them for the ears later.

STEP 4: Fold each of the pipe cleaner pieces in half, then poke them into the foam ball in a circle around the middle. Continue poking pieces into the foam until you've gone around the entire ball. Open each of the folded pipe cleaners into a rounded diamond shape.

STEP 5: Draw the face onto the lion using a black washable marker. Start by drawing a heart in the middle for the nose. Then draw a forward and backwards "J" shape down from the nose for the mouth. Finally, add 3 dots on both sides of the nose for the whiskers.

STEP 6: Apply crafter's tape to the back of the googly eyes and press them in position on the face.

Bend the 2 small pipe cleaner pieces that you saved in Step 3 into 2 small "U" shapes and press them into the top of the head for the ears.

STEP 7: Cut out a "U" shape from the top of the toilet paper roll, just big enough to hold the lion's head.

Place the lion's head into the opening and use tape to attach it to the inside of the paper roll to hold it in place.

STEP 8: Cut a short tail for the lion, about 2 inches (5 cm) long by ¼ inch (0.6 cm) wide. Attach the smallest pom pom to one end using crafter's tape. Tape the other end to the bottom middle at the back of the paper roll at a bit of an angle so you can see the tail from the front.

STEP 9: Use crafter's tape to attach the 2 medium pom poms as the lion's feet and the 2 small pom poms as the lion's arms.

Your paper roll lion is complete!

Foam Cup ♡ Zebra ♡

LEVEL OF DIFFICULTY 3/5 ✦ PARENTAL SUPERVISION NOT REQUIRED.

GET READY TO PRACTICE YOUR SCISSOR SKILLS! At the end of this craft you'll be a whiz at making construction paper hair. (Don't worry, it's easy!) Keep your hands clean by using strips of paper for your zebra stripes instead of paint or markers. This is another great time to use crafter's tape instead of drippy white glue!

I FIND THAT LIQUID CHALK MARKERS work the best to draw on black construction paper, but don't worry if you don't have any. You can also use a white crayon or pencil crayon to draw the nose and mouth. Just press a little harder than normal and go over it a few times to make the white a little brighter.

MATERIALS
- 2 pieces of construction paper (1 black, 1 white)
- Foam cup
- White liquid chalk marker (or white pencil crayon)
- 2 medium googly eyes

TOOLS
- Scissors
- Crafter's tape

STEP 1: Cut out a strip of black construction paper, about 2 inches (5 cm) wide. Then cut out 6 triangles across the rectangle so each triangle is about 2 inches (5 cm) long.

STEP 2: Attach the triangles to the foam cup using crafter's tape to make the zebra's stripes.

STEP 3: Cut out an oval shape from the black construction paper. Use the white chalk marker to draw a mouth and nose on it.

STEP 4: Apply crafter's tape to the back of the black oval and the back of the googly eyes and press them into position on the foam cup to make the zebra's face.

STEP 5: Cut out 2 smaller triangles from the black construction paper and use crafter's tape to attach them above the googly eyes as the zebra's eyebrows.

STEP 6: Cut out a rectangle from the black construction paper, about 2 inches (5 cm) wide and 3 inches (7.5 cm) tall. Cut a fringe into the rectangle on both of the long sides, being sure to leave a section uncut across the middle. Fold the fringe upwards.

Apply crafter's tape down the middle of the back of the black construction paper fringe and attach it to the back of the foam cup as the zebra's mane.

STEP 7: Cut out a smaller rectangle from the black construction paper, about 1 inch (2.5 cm) wide by ¾ inch (1.9 cm) tall. Cut a fringe into the long edge of the paper and bend it upwards.

Apply crafter's tape along the bottom fold of the fringe and attach it to the top of the head as the zebra's hair.

STEP 8: Cut out 2 ear shaped pieces from white construction paper. Then cut out 2 smaller ear shaped pieces from black construction paper. Use crafter's tape to attach the black ear pieces on top of the white ear pieces.

STEP 9: Make a small fold at the bottom of each ear. Apply crafter's tape to the bottom of the fold and attach the ears to the top of the cup.

STEP 10: Your foam cup zebra is complete!

Pipe Cleaner Monkey

LEVEL OF DIFFICULTY 5/5 + PARENTAL SUPERVISION NOT REQUIRED.

THESE LITTLE MONKEYS made from craft foam and pipe cleaners are so much fun. You can bend their arms to make them sit, hang them from things and most importantly make them hold onto their bananas. A monkey just isn't complete without a banana!

THESE MONKEYS CAN BE PUT TOGETHER entirely with crafter's tape. Which means there's zero glue needed! And even better, you don't have to wait for anything to dry. Apply the crafter's tape, press it to stick and you're ready to go!

MATERIALS
- 1 piece of craft foam (brown)
- 1 piece of thick paper (light brown)
- 4 pipe cleaners (3 brown and 1 yellow)
- 2 medium googly eyes

TOOLS
- Pencil
- Scissors
- Crafter's tape
- Washable marker (black)

STEP 1: On the brown craft foam, draw 2 small circle shapes (¾ inch [1.9 cm] across), one larger circle shape (1½ inches [3.8 cm]) across) and 2 identical oval shapes (2¾ inches [7 cm] long by 1½ inches [3.8 cm] across). Cut out all of the shapes.

On the thick light brown paper, draw 2 ovals (1½ inches [3.8 cm] long by 1 inch [2.5 cm] across) and one circle (a little less than 1.5 inches [3.8 cm] across). Cut out all of the shapes. Trim the circle piece so the top looks like the top of a heart shape.

STEP 2: Use crafter's tape to attach the rounded paper heart shape to the large craft foam circle.

Then use crafter's tape to attach one of the paper ovals on top of the rounded heart shape. Draw a nose and mouth onto the oval with the washable marker.

1

2

3

4

5

6

7

8

9

STEP 6: Use crafter's tape to attach the other paper oval to the front of the craft foam oval as the monkey's belly.

Add a short line of crafter's tape to the bottom of the back of the monkey's head and attach it to the front of the craft foam oval, pressing the craft foam to hold it in place.

Attach the googly eyes with the crafter's tape.

STEP 7: Cut the final brown pipe cleaner in half. Curl one end of one piece into a loose spiral shape. Save the other pipe cleaner half for another day.

STEP 8: Poke the straight end of the pipe cleaner into position on the back of the craft foam oval through one layer of craft foam for the monkey's tail.

Bend the pipe cleaner arms, legs and tail towards the front so your monkey can sit on its own.

STEP 9: Cut the yellow pipe cleaner in half. Bend one end of the pipe cleaner into a "J" shape. Save the other pipe cleaner half for another day.

Tightly wrap the yellow pipe cleaner back around the curve of the "J" shape until you reach the end. Trim off any extra pipe cleaner at the end. Place the pipe cleaner banana into your monkey's hand.

Your pipe cleaner monkey is complete!

STEP 3: Flip it over and use crafter's tape to attach the 2 small foam circles to the back of the large foam circle. These are the monkey's ears.

STEP 4: Bend one of the brown pipe cleaners in half. Bend each end of the pipe cleaner outwards and make a "W" shape. Twist each of the pipe cleaner ends back around the straight pipe cleaner to make the feet. Repeat with a second brown pipe cleaner.

These are the monkey's arms and legs so add another bend for the elbows and knees.

STEP 5: Apply a line of crafter's tape on the large craft foam oval near the top and bottom. Place the pipe cleaner arms and legs into position on top of the crafter's tape.

Apply crafter's tape to one side of the other large craft foam oval, then press it onto the oval shape with the pipe cleaner arms and legs. Press down on the oval to get the crafter's tape to stick.

> **HINT**: See if you can find household objects to trace for the foam shapes. Maybe a fat marker would work for the small circles? And a glue stick for the big circle? For the oval, you could try tracing a shampoo bottle or maybe a deodorant tube? Look around the house and see what you can find.

Pipe Cleaner Flamingo

LEVEL OF DIFFICULTY 4/5 ◆ PARENTAL SUPERVISION
ASK A GROWN UP TO HELP WITH THE GLUE GUN.

MY OLDEST DAUGHTER LOVES FLAMINGOES! Seriously—plates, shirts, decorations, stuffed animals, pajamas—if it has a flamingo on it, we have it somewhere in our house. They are such a fun and quirky animal!

THESE PIPE CLEANER FLAMINGOES are surprisingly simple to make. Bending and winding different colored pipe cleaners together is a great low-mess way to make all sorts of super awesome shapes and creatures. The more you can avoid glue and scissors, the less mess you'll make! The black and white pipe cleaner beak against the pink head looks so cool—just like a real flamingo's head.

MATERIALS
- 5 pipe cleaners (3 pink, 1 white and 1 black)
- 1 large pom pom (pink)
- 2 small googly eyes
- 2 craft feathers (pink)

TOOLS
- Scissors
- Low-temperature glue gun

STEP 1: Cut the black, white and one of the pink pipe cleaners in half. (Fold them in half to find the middle.) Keep one half of each color and save the other pieces for another day.

STEP 2: Take the black pipe cleaner half and fold the end in by about 1½ inches (3.8 cm).

Then start winding the white pipe cleaner tightly around the black pipe cleaner, leaving about ¼ inch (0.6 cm) of black showing at the folded end.

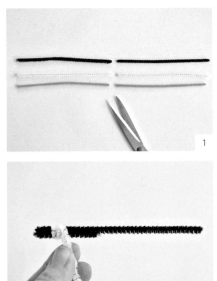

3

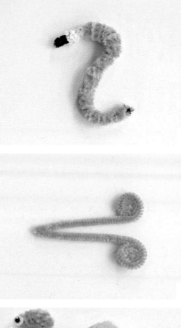

4

STEP 3: Leave about ¼ inch (0.6 cm) of white showing, then start winding one of the full length pink pipe cleaners tightly around the white and black pipe cleaners. Wind 2 layers of pink pipe cleaner around the first ¾ inch (1.9 cm), then wind in single layers until the pink pipe cleaner runs out.

Using the pink pipe cleaner half, continue winding around the black pipe cleaner until you reach the end.

5

STEP 4: Curve the pipe cleaner into an "S" shape to make the flamingo's head and neck.

STEP 5: Roll the pink pom pom between your hands to make it more of an oval shape.

STEP 6: Fold the last pink pipe cleaner in half. Bend both ends of the pipe cleaner outwards and roll them into 2 tight ½-inch (1.3-cm) wide spirals. Bend each of the spirals upwards to make the flamingo's feet.

6

7

8

STEP 7: Attach the googly eyes to the flamingo's head using a small dab of hot glue from the glue gun.

STEP 8: Attach the flamingo's head and feet to the pom pom using a hot glue gun. Use your fingers to spread apart the fluff in the pom pom and add a glob of hot glue deep in the opening. Then stick the pipe cleaner end into the glob of glue.

STEP 9: Add a small dab of hot glue to the tip of each pink feather, then press them into the front part of the pom pom near the neck, with the feather pointing towards the tail end of the flamingo.

STEP 10: Your pipe cleaner flamingo is complete!

9

10

Paper Roll Elephant

LEVEL OF DIFFICULTY 3/5 ◆ PARENTAL SUPERVISION
ASK A GROWN UP FOR HELP WITH CUTTING THE SLITS THROUGH THE TOILET PAPER ROLL.

WHO WOULD HAVE THOUGHT you could transform a simple paper roll into such a fun zoo animal?! Keep the mess to a minimum by covering the paper roll with construction paper instead of painting it. It's quick and easy and you don't have to wait for any paint to dry.

I ABSOLUTELY LOVE this elephant's ears. Just make sure you cut the openings in the paper tube large enough for the folded paper to fit through. If they are starting to rip and bend, the opening needs to be a little bigger.

MATERIALS
- 2 pieces of construction paper (light blue)
- 1 toilet paper roll
- 1 scrap of white paper
- 2 large googly eyes

TOOLS
- Scissors
- Tape
- Glue stick
- Pencil
- Washable marker (black)
- Crafter's tape

STEP 1: Cut out a rectangle of construction paper just large enough to cover the entire toilet paper roll. Use tape to attach one end of the construction paper to the paper roll. Apply glue to the entire inside surface of the paper with a glue stick, then roll it around the toilet paper roll, pressing it to the paper roll as you go.

STEP 2: Cut the corners off the second piece of construction paper to make a large oval shape.

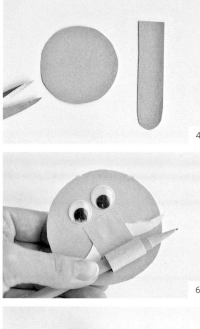

STEP 3: Fold the shorter edge of the oval upwards by about 1 inch (2.5 cm). Flip it over and fold it by another 1 inch (2.5 cm). Continue folding the paper evenly, back and forth in opposite directions, until you reach the end. These will be the elephant's ears.

STEP 4: Cut out a circle shape from the construction paper, about 2¾ inches (7 cm) wide. Trace a small bowl or foam cup to help with the shape. Cut out a long rectangle shape from the construction paper, about 4 inches (10 cm) long and 1 inch (2.5 cm) wide. Trim off the corners from one end of the rectangle to curve one end.

STEP 5: Cut out 2 tusk shapes from the scrap of white paper, about 1¼ inches (3 cm) long. Attach the tusks near the middle of the construction paper circle using a glue stick.

Then attach the long rectangular piece over the top of the tusks using a glue stick with the curved end pointing downwards.

STEP 6: Apply crafter's tape to the back of each googly eye and press them into position on the elephant's face.

Roll the elephant's trunk tightly around a round pencil to curve the paper. (Make sure the pencil is round without any corners or ridges around it or you'll see them when you roll the paper.)

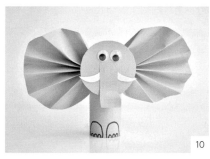

STEP 7: Cut a slit, approximately 1¼ inches (3 cm) wide, in both sides of the paper roll. Make sure it's just large enough to fit the folded elephant ears. Be sure to position the slits so that the paper seam is at the back.

STEP 8: Carefully push the folded elephant ears through each of the slits. Pull them through the paper roll so that the ears are centered on both sides.

Draw 2 elephant feet on the bottom edge of the paper roll. For each of the feet, draw one large upside down "U" shape, with 3 evenly spaced small upside down "U" shapes along the bottom.

STEP 9: Spread open the folds in the ear and use a glue stick to attach the bottom and top fold of each side to the paper roll. Then use a glue stick to attach the head to the front of the elephant.

STEP 10: Your paper roll elephant is complete!

Paper Roll Giraffe

LEVEL OF DIFFICULTY 4/5 ✦ PARENTAL SUPERVISION NOT REQUIRED.

MATERIALS
- 1 toilet paper roll
- 2 pieces of construction paper (1 yellow and 1 brown)
- 2 small googly eyes
- 4 craft sticks

TOOLS
- Scissors
- Washable marker (brown)
- Glue stick
- Pencil

GIRAFFES ARE SUCH COOL ANIMALS. I find their long necks so fascinating. When my kids were babies, they had a stuffed giraffe that stood on the dresser in their nursery—it still lives in my son's bedroom. This craft reminds me of that stuffed giraffe, with skinny legs that make it stand proud and tall.

USING BRIGHT AND COLORFUL PAPER is an awesome low-mess alternative to painting when you're crafting. But don't forget that you can add even more color by using washable markers on the paper too! Coloring your giraffe spots on with markers is much easier (and tidier!) than cutting out little circles of paper and gluing them on.

STEP 1: Cut the toilet paper roll to be about 3½ inches (8.9 cm) long.

Cut out a rectangle of yellow construction paper just large enough to cover the trimmed toilet paper roll. Color oval shaped spots all over the rectangle with brown washable marker.

Apply glue to the entire inside surface of the construction paper with a glue stick, then roll it around the toilet paper roll, pressing it to the paper roll as you go.

STEP 2: Fold a rectangular scrap of yellow construction paper over by about 2 inches (5 cm). Draw a giraffe head shape onto the folded paper. Cut the shape out from the folded paper so you end up with 2 identical giraffe head shapes.

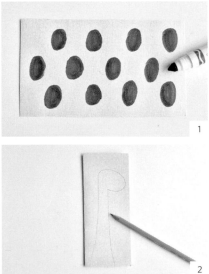

STEP 3: Draw oval shaped spots all over the neck of the giraffe with brown washable marker. Draw 2 dots for the nose and a short little smile.

STEP 4: Cut a long rectangular strip of brown construction paper 6 inches (15 cm) long by ¾ inch (1.9 cm) wide. Cut a fringe into one side of the long rectangle by making cuts very close together along the long edge edge.

Cut a short piece, about ¾ inch (1.9 cm) long off the end of the long rectangular fringe.

Cut 2 small ear shapes from yellow construction paper.

STEP 5: Attach the googly eyes to the giraffe's face using a glue stick.

Attach the long rectangular fringe piece to the inside of the other giraffe head piece using a glue stick, with the fringe pointing out from the neck. Then attach the shorter fringe piece and the ears to the top of the head using a glue stick.

Cover the whole piece with glue from the glue stick. Line up the giraffe head pieces and press them together.

STEP 6: Cut 4 slits in the bottom of the toilet paper roll, about ½ inch (1.3 cm) away from the paper seam on both sides.

Cut a larger slit in the top middle of the paper roll, long enough to fit the bottom of the giraffe's neck. Make sure the top slit is centered above the slits below it.

STEP 7: Color one end of each craft stick brown to make the giraffe's hooves.

STEP 8: Cut out a long skinny rectangle of yellow construction paper, about 3 inches (7.5 cm) long and ¼ inch (0.6 cm) wide. Color one end of the rectangle brown, then cut short slits into it to make the tail.

STEP 9: Slide the giraffe's head into the slit on the top of the paper roll. Slide a craft stick into each of the 4 slits on the bottom of the paper roll.

Attach the tail to the back of the paper roll at the top middle using a glue stick.

STEP 10: Your paper roll giraffe is complete!

Mini Paper Penguins

LEVEL OF DIFFICULTY 2/5 ✦ PARENTAL SUPERVISION NOT REQUIRED.

THESE TINY LITTLE ZOO ANIMALS are so sweet and they are quick and easy to put together. Everything is more fun when it's mini, don't you think? I tried making these penguins much larger at first (give it a try!), but I found they looked so much better when they fit in the palm of my hand.

YOU ONLY NEED 4 THINGS FOR THIS CRAFT—construction paper, googly eyes, scissors and a glue stick. Cleaning up is so easy when you're only using a few simple supplies! I recommend making these guys just large enough to fit over your fingers. Then, after you're done waddling them across the floor, you can slide them onto your fingers and put on a little penguin puppet show!

STEP 1: Cut out a rectangle from the black construction paper, about 3.5 inches (9 cm) wide and 2 inches (5 cm) tall.

Apply glue to the inside edge using a glue stick, then roll the rectangle into a tube shape.

STEP 2: For the penguin's feet, cut out a rectangle of orange construction paper, about ½ inch (1.3 cm) wide and 1 inch (2.5 cm) tall. Trim the corners off one end and cut a triangle from the middle so the end looks like 2 side by side triangles.

For the penguin's beak, cut out a long triangle from orange construction paper.

For the penguin's belly, cut a rectangle, about ½ inch (1.3 cm) wide and ¾ inch (1.9 cm) tall. Trim the corners off one end to make it curved.

STEP 3: Attach the rounded white belly piece to the front middle of the black paper roll using a glue stick.

Make a small fold in the wide end of the orange triangle. Add glue to the back of the fold using a glue stick and attach it to the middle of the black paper roll, just above the white belly piece.

STEP 4: Attach the googly eyes above the penguins beak using a glue stick.

Add glue to one side of the orange rectangle feet using a glue stick and slide it inside of the paper roll with the glued side facing towards the front of the penguin. Press the orange rectangle piece to the inside of the black paper roll. Bend the feet towards the front of the penguin.

STEP 5: Cut a fringe in the top of the penguins head by making short slits, very close together, around the entire top edge.

STEP 6: Your mini paper penguin is complete!

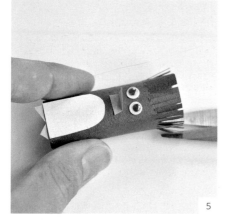

Folded Paper Peacock

LEVEL OF DIFFICULTY 2/5 ✦ PARENTAL SUPERVISION NOT REQUIRED.

MATERIALS

- 1 piece of self-adhesive sparkly blue craft foam
- 1 scrap of construction paper (yellow)
- 2 medium googly eyes
- 2 pipe cleaners (6" [15.3 cm] length, dark blue)
- 1 piece of construction paper (green)
- Sticker rhinestones (silver)

TOOLS

- Pencil
- Scissors
- Crafter's tape
- Washable markers (yellow, blue and green)

HAVE YOU EVER SEEN a peacock in real life? Or even just a peacock feather? The colors and shapes are really beautiful. And when a peacock opens its feathers and struts along, it's absolutely stunning! They look like royalty.

GLITTER FOAM IS A FANTASTIC WAY to make your crafts sparkle without having to deal with a messy jar of glitter. Use self-adhesive glitter foam and self-adhesive rhinestone stickers to decorate the feathery tail. There's no glue needed for this sparkly little peacock!

STEP 1: On the back of the sparkly blue craft foam, draw a bird head shape and cut it out.

STEP 2: Fold the scrap of yellow construction paper. Cut out a triangle on the fold so it opens up like a long diamond and folds in half to look like a beak.

Apply the crafter's tape to the back of the googly eyes and the bottom half of the beak and attach them to the peacock's face on the front of the blue craft foam.

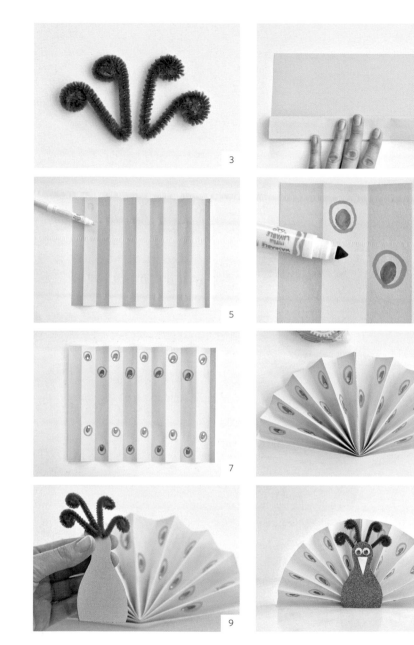

STEP 3: Fold each of the 6-inch (15-cm) long pipe cleaners in half into a "V" shape. If you only have long pipe cleaners, cut one in half to get two 6-inch (15-cm) pieces.

Pinch each of the pipe cleaner ends and curl them into a tight spiral, with both spirals going out towards the same side.

STEP 4: Using the entire sheet of green construction paper, fold the shorter edge upwards by about 1 inch (2.5 cm). Flip it over and fold it upwards by another 1 inch (2.5 cm). Continue folding the paper evenly, back and forth in opposite directions, until you reach the end.

STEP 5: Open the paper back up and lay it flat.

Using a yellow washable marker, draw an incomplete circle, with the bottom open (almost like a horseshoe shape) on the outer edge of each of the folds on both long edges of the paper.

STEP 6: Color a blue circle in the middle of each of the yellow circle shapes.

Draw a green circle around the outside of each of the yellow and blue circle shapes.

STEP 7: Press a silver rhinestone sticker at the bottom of each of the blue circles.

STEP 8: Fold the paper back up again. Then fold it in half to make a shorter rectangle, pinching the fold to make a crease.

Line up the 2 edges of paper that come together in the middle of the fan shape and tape them together using crafter's tape.

STEP 9: Peel the backing off of the self-adhesive craft foam. Press the pipe cleaner "feathers" onto the sticky part of the foam on the top of the head.

Press the peacock head into the bottom middle of the peacock tail shape, carefully pressing the sticky part to the folds in the fanned tail.

STEP 10: Your folded paper peacock is complete!

Chapter 5

Little Monsters
PUPPET SHOW

Lights. Camera. Action! Now you can put on the funniest, most awesome puppet show in the history of puppet shows. Puppets are so much fun to make and even more fun to play with. Practice your different monster voices, because this quirky little troop of characters is going to get everyone at home laughing!

≫ LOW-MESS TIP: ONLY PULL OUT WHAT YOU'RE GOING TO USE ≪

Try to get in the habit of only bringing materials to the table if you are going to use them. For example, in this chapter when you're making the Fuzzy Friend Sock Puppet (page 90), only pull out 2 googly eyes, instead of the whole bag. And when you're making the Wiggly Worm Puppet (page 88), count out exactly 13 small pom poms, instead of bringing your whole pom pom collection.

Go through the materials list when you start a new craft and collect exactly what you are going to need, similar to how you would only pull out the ingredients you needed if you were going to bake a cake. When you use up all the materials that you've pulled out, you don't have to put them away.
And that makes cleaning up quick and easy!

Wiggly Worm Puppet (page 88), Fuzzy Friend Sock Puppet (page 90), Simple Folded Paper Puppets (page 92), Pom Pom Hand Puppets (page 94), Winter Glove Monster Puppet (page 96), Rubber Glove Dragon Puppet (page 98), Dancing Ostrich Marionette (page 100), Pipe Cleaner Finger Puppets (page 102)

≡ Wiggly Worm ≡ Puppet

LEVEL OF DIFFICULTY 3/5 ◆ PARENTAL SUPERVISION
ASK A GROWN UP TO HELP WITH THE NEEDLE AND THREAD.

OUT OF ALL THE CRAFTS IN THIS BOOK, this one was my very favorite. It's so simple to make and the little worms just come to life! The way they wiggle and squirm makes me smile every single time. And they're the perfect craft to try if you're just learning to use a marionette.

ITS ALWAYS TEMPTING to empty out your whole craft bin when you're making something, but I recommend only pulling out exactly what you need for this craft and then putting the bin away before you start (so get counting those pom poms!). When you get in the habit of gathering just what you need, there's no leftover pieces to worry about and it makes it super simple to tidy up when you're done!

MATERIALS
- Thread
- Sewing needle
- 13 small pom poms
- Craft stick
- Small googly eyes

TOOLS
- Scissors
- Crafter's tape

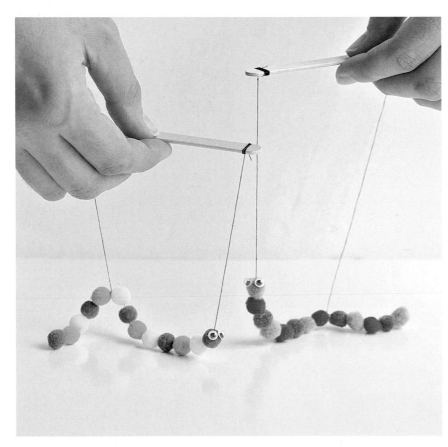

STEP 1: Cut a piece of thread, about 18 inches (46 cm) long. Tie a knot at one end and thread the other end through the hole in the sewing needle.

STEP 2: Push the needle through the middle of each pom pom and slide them down the thread all the way to the knot at the end.

3

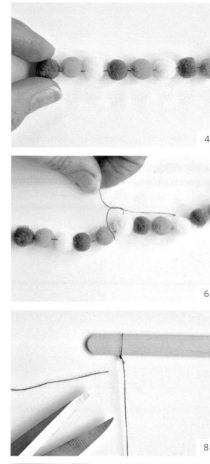

4

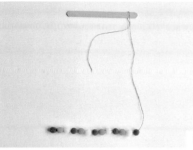

5

6

7

8

9

10

STEP 3: Keep adding pom poms until you've added all of them. Remove the sewing needle. Make sure you put it away carefully so it doesn't fall onto the floor!

STEP 4: Holding the pom pom closest to the knot at the end, gently pull away each of the pom poms so there is a small space between every single pom pom.

STEP 5: Tie the thread around one end of the craft stick and into a knot.

STEP 6: Cut another piece of thread, about 12 inches (30.5 cm) long. Loop this piece of thread around the space just after the fifth pom pom from the end with the knot. Tie it into a knot tightly around the thread.

STEP 7: Making sure the front and back strings are the same length, tie the end of the thread around the other end of the craft stick.

STEP 8: Trim off the extra thread from the 2 knots on the craft stick and the knot around the thread in between the pom poms.

STEP 9: Apply crafter's tape to the back of the googly eyes and attach them to the front pom pom. (The front pom pom is the one with the thread coming out of it.)

STEP 10: Your wiggly worm puppet is complete!

Fuzzy Friend Sock Puppet

LEVEL OF DIFFICULTY 4/5 ⧫ PARENTAL SUPERVISION
ASK A GROWN UP TO HELP WITH THE GLUE GUN.

DON'T LET THIS PUPPET FOOL YOU—it's simple to make! And there's no sewing required. The key is to find a soft and fuzzy sock to use. I found these socks at the dollar store.

FOR SOCK PUPPETS, it's all about the hair. You can definitely make a wig with yarn or felt, but it's so much easier (and less messy!) to use a curly gift wrapping bow instead! You can find them in lots of stores in the gift wrapping section and they come ready made with oodles of dangling curls in all the colors of the rainbow.

STEP 1: On the back side of the self-adhesive craft foam, trace around a round object, such as a foam cup or a drinking cup, with a pencil. Cut out the circle shape from the red craft foam and fold the foam circle in half.

Cut out a small tongue shape from the pink construction paper.

STEP 2: Attach the tongue shape to the inside of the foam circle mouth using crafter's tape.

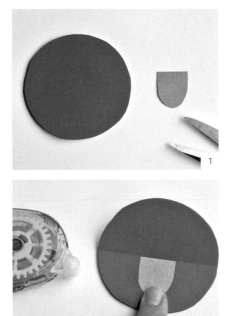

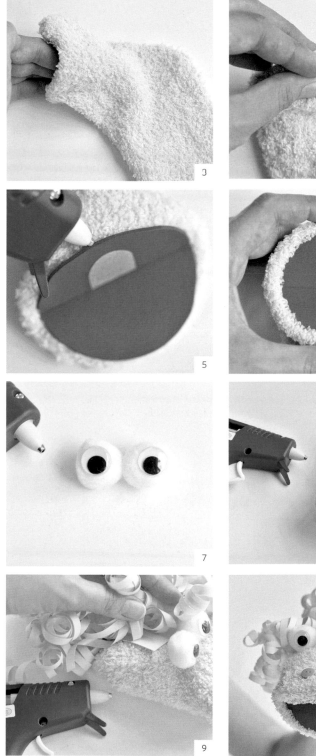

STEP 3: Put the sock over one of your hands so that your fingers go all the way to the end. Using the fingers of your other hand, push the tip of the sock inside by about 2 inches (5 cm), as if you were starting to turn the sock inside out.

STEP 4: With your hand still in the sock, slide the folded circle of craft foam into the opening in the sock and hold it in place with your fingers inside the sock.

Carefully remove the entire backing from the self-adhesive craft foam circle and use your fingers inside the sock to press the sticky foam onto the sock.

STEP 5: Take your hand out of the sock. Apply a line of hot glue, about 1 inch (2.5 cm) long, to the edge of the foam circle. Pull the sock up and slightly over the outer edge of the circle and press it onto the hot glue and hold it for about 15 seconds, or until it dries.

STEP 6: Slowly work your way around the entire edge of the foam circle, applying about 1 inch (2.5 cm) of hot glue to the edge at a time, then pulling the sock over the top and pressing it onto the hot glue.

Continue until you've glued around the edge of the entire foam circle.

STEP 7: Attach the googly eyes to the white pom poms using a glue gun.

STEP 8: Attach the pom pom eyes and 2 buttons for the nose to the puppet's head using a glue gun.

STEP 9: Attach the curly ribbon gift wrapping bow to the top of the puppet's head using a glue gun.

STEP 10: Your fuzzy friend sock puppet is complete!

Simple Folded Paper Puppets

SLIDE YOUR FINGERS AND THUMB into the little pockets at the top and bottom of these folded paper puppets to bring them to life! My 2-year-old son picked up one of these puppets and shocked us with his amazing monster voice. And then he burst out laughing that we were laughing. And pretty soon everyone in the house was laughing!

ITS AMAZING WHAT YOU CAN CREATE from just a few simple sheets of brightly colored paper. Keep the scraps under control by cutting over the top of a large placemat or baking sheet. It makes it so easy to gather up all the little pieces and makes cleaning up simple!

MATERIALS
- 2 pieces of paper (1 light green and 1 dark green)
- 4 scraps of construction paper (white, pink, black and red)

TOOLS
- Scissors
- Washable marker (black)
- Glue stick

STEP 1: Take the long edge of the light green paper and fold it approximately to the middle.

STEP 2: Take the other long edge and fold it so it just overlaps the other edge that's been folded in.

3

4

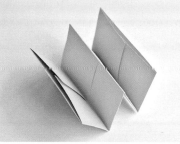

5

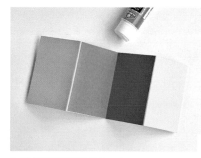

7

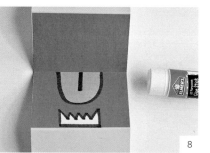

8

9

10

STEP 3: Flip the folded paper over so that the overlapping edges are on the bottom. Fold the rectangular piece in half to make a shorter rectangle.

STEP 4: Take the top piece of the folded paper and fold it in half so the edge lines up with the middle fold.

STEP 5: Flip it over and do the same to the other side. When you let go, the paper should look like a folded "W" shape.

Your fingers will go into the opening at the top of the "W" and your thumb will go into the opening at the bottom of the "W".

STEP 6: Cut out eyes, eyebrows, a nose, a tongue and teeth from construction paper. Draw around the edge of each piece with the black washable marker.

STEP 7: Cut out a rectangle of red construction paper to fit between the middle 2 folds in the folded paper puppet shape. Fold the red rectangle in half, then attach it to the folded paper puppet shape using a glue stick.

STEP 8: Attach the tongue and the teeth to the bottom part of the red rectangle using a glue stick.

STEP 9: Cut out a head for the puppet from the darker green paper. Give it rounded, curved or zigzag edges. Attach it at the top of the puppet using a glue stick.

Glue the eyes, eyebrows and nose into position on the head using a glue stick.

STEP 10: Your simple folded paper puppet is complete!

HINT: Running low on paper colors? No problem! Instead of cutting out all the shapes, use markers to draw and color the face and mouth of your puppet!

Pom Pom Hand Puppets

LEVEL OF DIFFICULTY 2/5 + PARENTAL SUPERVISION
ASK A GROWN UP TO HELP WITH THE GLUE GUN.

WHO NEEDS A FANCY PUPPET when you can use your hand?! Slide your middle finger into one of these pom pom hand puppets and use your fingers and thumb as the mouth. Hands can be surprisingly funny when you make them talk in a silly voice!

DO YOU WANT ANOTHER LOW-MESS CRAFT TIP? Look for bags of short pipe cleaners to add to your craft stash. There's no scraps to worry about when you don't have to cut anything. Try curling a short pipe cleaner into a spiral for one set of eyes. Or use sparkly pom poms to make eyelashes on another one. A small change can inspire a completely new personality for your puppet.

STEP 1: Fold one of the pipe cleaners in half, then bend it into a "U" shape.

STEP 2: Spread apart the fluff in one of the large pom poms. Add a small glob of hot glue into the opening, then press one of the the pipe cleaner ends into the glue, pushing the fluff of the pom pom back into place around the pipe cleaner.

Repeat with the other end of the pipe cleaner with the second large pom pom.

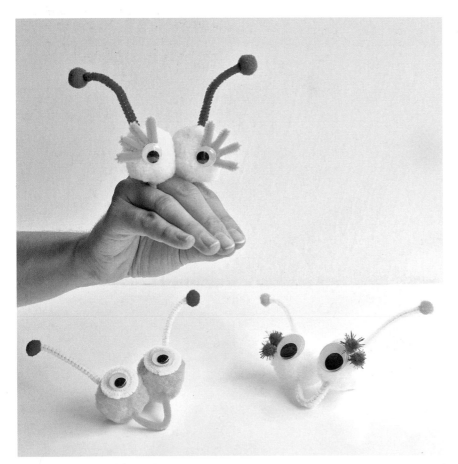

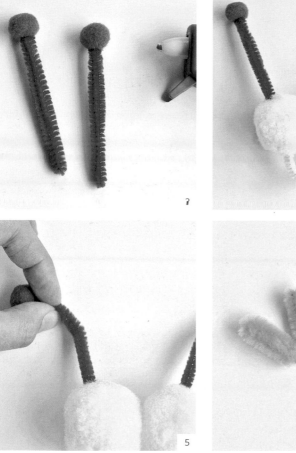

STEP 3: Fold 2 pipe cleaners in half. Add a small dab of hot glue onto the small pom poms and press them onto the tip of each pipe cleaner half. These will be the antennae.

STEP 4: Attach the pipe cleaner antennae to the top of each of the large pom poms using a glue gun.

STEP 5: Bend the pipe cleaner antennae slightly so they curve.

STEP 6 Take the end of another pipe cleaner and fold the end by about ½ inch (1.3 cm). Fold it by ½ inch (1.3 cm) in the other direction. Continue folding it back and forth, in opposite directions, until you get to the end. Repeat for the last pipe cleaner. These will be the puppet's eyebrows.

STEP 7: Attach the eyebrows to the front of the large pom poms using hot glue.

Then attach the googly eyes slighly over the top of the eyebrows, again using hot glue.

STEP 8: Your pom pom hand puppet is complete!

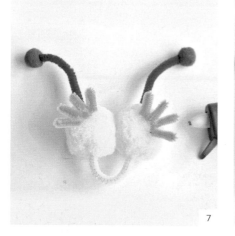

Winter Glove Monster Puppet

LEVEL OF DIFFICULTY 1/5 ✦ PARENTAL SUPERVISION
ASK A GROWN UP TO HELP WITH THE GLUE GUN.

MATERIALS
* 1 small scrap of long hair fur (about 2 x 4" [5 x 10 cm])
* 1 winter glove
* 2 large googly eyes
* 7 medium googly eyes

TOOLS
* Scissors
* Low-temperature glue gun

YOU CAN FIND LONG HAIR FUR at any fabric store, and most craft stores. If you have trouble finding the color you want, try looking in the stuffed animal section at the dollar store. A crafty grown up might be willing to help you remove the fur by cutting along the seams or using a seam ripper.

THIS IS SUCH A FUN CRAFT PROJECT that only uses a handful of materials! The only scraps you'll be making are from cutting the scraps of long hair fur. I recommend cutting the fur over the top of a large placemat or baking sheet to make it easier to collect and throw away any of the stray fur bits that may fall off. It makes cleaning up easy!

STEP 1: Cut out 5 small strips of fur, about a ½ inch (1.3 cm) wide and 2 inches (5 cm) long each. The fur needs to be wide enough to wrap around a finger. Cut as close to the bottom of the fabric as possible and pull the long fur out of the way of the scissors so you don't trim it off.

STEP 2: Add a small line of hot glue to one end of a fur strip, then overlap the other end on top, pressing it onto the glue, to make a small circle. Repeat for the other 4 strips of fur.

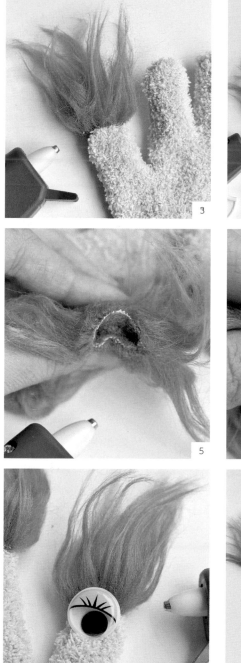

STEP 3: Add a small line of hot glue around the inside bottom edge of one of the fur pieces. Press it onto the tip of one of the fingers of the winter glove.

STEP 4: Repeat for the other 4 fingers of the glove so that each glove finger has fur on the tip.

STEP 5: Gently pull the fur on each finger downwards so you can see the circle opening.

STEP 6: Add a small line of glue into the opening then pinch the opening closed.

Repeat for the other 4 fingers of the glove.

STEP 7: Decide which googly eyes you want on which finger, then attach them to the glove using the glue gun. Glue each eye on the edge of the fur so that they are half on the glove and half on the fur.

STEP 8: Your winter glove monster puppet is complete!

Rubber Glove Dragon Puppet

LEVEL OF DIFFICULTY 4/5 ✦ PARENTAL SUPERVISION
ASK A GROWN UP TO HELP WITH THE GLUE GUN AND CRAFT KNIFE.

I NAMED THIS DRAGON HARRY. And Harry is absolutely full of personality. I think it's his hair? He looks like the type of dragon that would nod his head and call you "bro." (He's a very friendly dragon.)

THIS IS A GREAT CRAFT WITH VERY FEW SCRAPS! Try to make the yarn hair the exact size you need so you don't need to give it a "haircut." If the yarn hair ends up being too long, don't worry! You can keep the mess to a minimum by trimming it over the top of a large placemat, baking sheet or even right over top of the trash can.

STEP 1: Carefully cut the foam ball in half using a craft knife.

Draw and color in 2 partial circles at the bottom of each foam ball half using the black permanent marker.

STEP 2: Attach the foam ball halves to the top of the rubber glove using the glue gun.

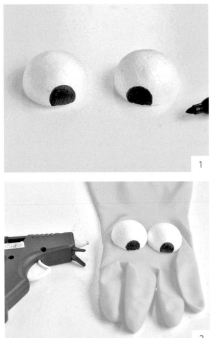

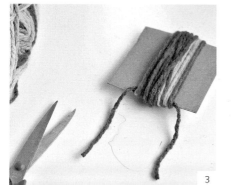

STEP 3: Wind the yarn around the piece of cardboard about 15 to 30 times. (The more times you wrap around, the more hair your puppet will have!) Cut the yarn when you're done winding.

Cut another piece of yarn about 6 inches (15 cm) long. Slide the 6-inch (15-cm) piece of yarn under the wound layers of yarn.

STEP 4: Tie it into a very tight knot. Then carefully slide the yarn off the cardboard.

Cut the yarn, directly opposite the knot so each side is the same length.

STEP 5: Attach the hair to the top of the head, right behind the foam eyes, using the glue gun.

STEP 6: Attach the 2 small pom poms to the end of the middle 2 fingers of the rubber glove using a glue gun.

STEP 7: Cut a tongue shape from the red craft foam.

Cut the dragon's pointy scales from the yellow craft foam. Make cuts along the flat edge of the yellow scales, about ½ inch (1.3 cm) deep and spaced ½ inch (1.3 cm) apart.

STEP 8: Attach the scales to the back of the rubber glove using a glue gun. Start behind the hair and work your way towards the end of the rubber glove.

STEP 9: Attach the tongue to the bottom of the glove, in the middle of the palm using a glue gun.

STEP 10: Your rubber glove dragon puppet is complete!

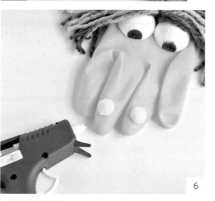

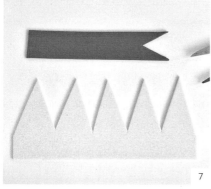

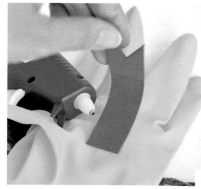

HINT: Rubber gloves can be tricky to work with. If you're having trouble getting things to stick using a glue gun, you might need to try using a stronger adhesive. Super glue should work or you can try E6000 craft adhesive. Start with the glue gun, and only use something stronger if you need to. It will depend on the type of rubber in your gloves.

Dancing Ostrich ✦ Marionette ✦

LEVEL OF DIFFICULTY 5/5 ✦ PARENTAL SUPERVISION
ASK A PARENT FOR HELP WITH THE GLUE GUN AND WITH THE NEEDLE AND THREAD.

YOU'LL NEED TO TURN ON SOME MUSIC for this silly ostrich, because she's got some moves! Her head bobs, her feet tap, and her feathers wiggle up and down. This is a more advanced marionette though, so I recommend making the wiggly worm puppet from earlier in this chapter before you try this one, just to get some practice working with marionette strings.

IT'S WELL WORTH IT THOUGH, because this silly girl (or you can easily make a boy) is lots of fun! Make sure you gather all the materials you're going to use before you get started. As long as you organize your materials first, it's easy to clean this one up since there's barely any scraps!

MATERIALS
- Ribbon
- 4 sparkly pom poms (1 large, 3 medium)
- Scrap of paper (orange)
- 2 medium googly eyes
- 2 small craft feathers
- 2 glass beads
- Thread
- Sewing needle
- 2 craft sticks

TOOLS
- Scissors
- Low-temperature glue gun

STEP 1: Cut 2 pieces of ribbon, about 3½ inches (9 cm) long.

Cut one piece of ribbon, about 2½ inches (6.5 cm) long.

Attach one end of each piece of ribbon to the 3 medium sparkly pom poms using a glue gun. The short one will be the ostrich's head and neck. The longer 2 will be the ostrich's legs.

STEP 2: Attach each of the ribbon ends of the 2 leg pieces to the bottom of the large sparkly pom pom using a glue gun.

Attach the ribbon end of the neck piece to the front of the large pom pom.

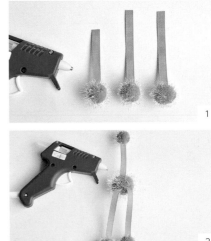

3

4

5

6

7

8

9

Repeat for the body, pushing the needle at an angle through the bottom of the large pom pom body so that the thread comes out at the very top between the neck and the feather tail.

Repeat for the head, pushing the needle at an angle through the pom pom so the thread comes out towards the back of the head behind the feather.

Carefully put the sewing needle away, making sure it doesn't fall onto the floor.

STEP 7: Straighten out the ostrich's head and legs into the proper position. Then take each piece of thread and pull it upwards.

STEP 8: Glue the 2 craft sticks together in a cross shape using a glue gun.

Lay the craft stick cross about 8 inches (20 cm) above the ostrich, depending on how long you want the strings to be. Tie the thread from the ostrich's head around the front end of the horizontal craft stick and secure it with a knot. Then tie the thread from the ostrich's tail around the back end of the horizontal craft stick and secure it with a knot.

Tie the thread from the ostrich's left leg around the top end of the vertical craft stick. Next, tie the thread from the ostrich's right leg around the bottom end of the vertical craft stick.

STEP 9: Lift up the craft stick cross. Adjust the lengths of the thread pieces if you need to to make sure the ostrich hangs properly. Trim off any extra thread. Once you've tied the thread to the craft stick, dab a small amount of hot glue onto each of the knots. This will help strengthen the knot and make sure it doesn't come untied later.

Your dancing ostrich marionette is complete!

STEP 3: Fold the scrap of orange paper in half. Cut a triangle on the fold (it should open up to look like a long diamond) to make the ostrich's beak.

Attach the googly eyes and the paper beak to the pom pom head using a glue gun.

STEP 4: Attach the larger feather in the back of the large pom pom using a glue gun. Then attach the smaller feather in the top of the pom pom head using a glue gun.

STEP 5: Attach the glass beads to the bottom of the pom pom feet using a glue gun. Having trouble finding glass beads? You can use metal washers or buttons to weigh down the feet instead.

STEP 6: Cut 4 pieces of thread, about 14 inches (36 cm) long each. Thread one through the eye of the sewing needle. Tie a knot at the other end.

Push the sewing needle through the bottom of the pom pom foot at an angle so the thread comes out on the top of the pom pom in front of the ribbon. Pull the thread all the way through the pom pom until the knot is hidden inside the pom pom. Remove the sewing needle from the thread and repeat with another piece of knotted thread for the other foot.

Pipe Cleaner Finger Puppets

LEVEL OF DIFFICULTY 2/5 ✦ PARENTAL SUPERVISION
ASK A GROWN UP FOR HELP WITH THE GLUE GUN.

MATERIALS
- 6 pipe cleaners
- 5 medium pom poms
- 10 googly eyes

TOOLS
- Low-temperature glue gun

POM POMS AND PIPE CLEANERS and googly eyes, oh my! These adorable little finger puppets are super simple to make. This is a great low-mess craft that needs zero cuts and makes zero scraps. Just a couple dabs of glue and you're done!

I FIRST MADE THESE FOR MY KIDS before my son was born and when my girls weren't old enough to go to school. They loved them! My younger daughter, who was only a year old at the time, was so proud just to be able to put them on her fingers. Even now, when we made them again, all three kids were super excited to test out this collection of finger puppet characters.

STEP 1: Wind one of the pipe cleaners around your finger 3 or 4 times.

STEP 2: For shorter ears, wind the pipe cleaner around your finger 4 times. Take the long end of the pipe cleaner and bend it straight up. Bend the pipe cleaner into a small "8" shape and twist the end around the middle to hold it in place.

3

4

STEP 3: Bend the small loops upwards slightly to make an ear shape.

STEP 4: For longer ears, wind the pipe cleaner around your finger 3 times before bending the end into ears.

STEP 5: Make a finger puppet with pointy ears.

STEP 6: Make a finger puppet with arms instead of ears.

STEP 7: Make a finger puppet with arms, like in Step 6. Then bend a second pipe cleaner into an "8" shape and twist it onto the middle of the arms.

STEP 8: Attach the pom poms to the top of each spiral using a glue gun.

STEP 9: Attach the googly eyes to each of the pom poms using a glue gun.

STEP 10: Your pipe cleaner finger puppets are complete!

5

6

7

8

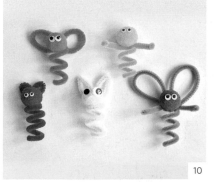

9

10

Chapter 6

On the ROAD

After this chapter, you're going to be an expert at making road vehicles! Get ready to raid the recycling bin, because these awesome little projects are going to upcycle some great materials that you never thought of using for crafting! Wheels that turn, how cool is that!?

≫ LOW-MESS TIP: PRE-MAKE YOURSELF "CRAFT KITS" ≪

I've talked about how important it is to organize your craft materials, but what if you take it one step further? Pick your favorite crafts in this chapter (maybe the Paper Roll Cars [page 106], the Shampoo Bottle Gas Station [page 112] and the 2D Wheelie Police Cars [page 114]?), and collect all the craft materials you'll need for each one. Then put all the materials needed to make one craft in a plastic zip bag. You could make a "craft kit" for most of the projects in this book, so make as many as you can!

Then when you're ready to do a little crafting, all you have to do is pull out a zip bag with the craft supplies inside and grab the box of craft tools (that was the one with scissors, tape, glue, markers, etc. that we talked about at the beginning of Chapter 3 [page 51]). Not only does it make it really quick to get started, it also makes cleaning up super easy since you didn't pull out any extra materials!

Paper Roll Cars (page 106), Candy Box Traffic Lights (page 108), Tissue Box Fire Truck (page 110), Shampoo Bottle Gas Station (page 112), 2D Wheelie Police Car (page 114), Simple Paper Street Signs (page 116), Poster Board Road Track (page 118), Snowy Mountain Cardboard Tunnel (page 120)

Paper Roll Cars

LEVEL OF DIFFICULTY 3/5 + PARENTAL SUPERVISION NOT REQUIRED.

START SAVING THOSE EMPTY TOILET PAPER ROLLS, because these cars are so much fun! Choose your colors, add racing stripes, and when you're done, you can race them across the floor—the wheels even spin! Using shiny wrapping paper and sparkly washi tape is a simple, low-mess way to customize your cars!

JUST MAKE SURE you use a drinking straw that fits easily through the hole of a single hole punch so that the wheels can turn. If you have trouble finding a small enough straw, try using 2 juice box straws. (Just make sure you wash and dry them first!)

MATERIALS
- Toilet paper roll
- 2 pieces of thick paper (1 white and 1 black)
- Scrap of shiny wrapping paper
- 1 drinking straw
- Sparkly washi tape

TOOLS
- Pencil
- Scissors
- Single hole punch
- Washable marker (black)
- Tape
- Crafter's tape

STEP 1: Trace around the edge of the toilet paper roll with a pencil to make 4 circles on the thick black paper.

Trace around a smaller circle (maybe the inner circle of the washi tape? Or a glue stick?) with a pencil to make 5 smaller circles on the thick white paper.

Cut out each of the circles. Punch a hole in the middle of each black circle using the single hole punch. Draw a number on one of the white circles, and draw a steering wheel onto another white circle using the black washable marker.

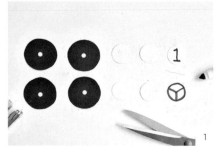

2

3

4

5

6

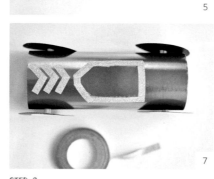

7

8

9

STEP 3: Cut the straw into 2 pieces, about 2.5 inches (6.5 cm) long each. Using scissors, carefully snip 4 small cuts into one end of each straw, about ¼ inch (0.6 cm) long each. Bend back the flaps at the end of each straw to make a cross shape.

Push the straw through the hole in one of the black circles. Cut a small piece of tape and press it onto the cross in the straw, pushing it onto the black paper so the tape holds the straw tightly. Repeat for the second straw in another black circle.

STEP 4: Apply crafter's tape to one side of one of the blank white circles and press it firmly onto the middle of the black circle, covering the taped end of the straw. Repeat for the second straw.

STEP 5: Slide one of the straws through the 2 holes at the front of the paper roll and slide the second straw through the 2 holes at the back of the paper roll.

STEP 6: Push one of the black circles onto each of the straw ends. Using scissors, carefully snip 4 small cuts into one end of each straw, just as you did in Step 3.

Bend back the flaps at the end of each straw to make a cross shape. Cut a small piece of tape and press it onto the cross in the straw, pushing it onto the black paper so the tape holds the straw tightly. Repeat for the second straw.

STEP 7: Apply crafter's tape to one side of one of the blank white circles and press it firmly onto the middle of the black circle, covering the taped end of the straw. Repeat for the second straw.

If the opening you cut on the top of the car looks a little messy, cover the cut edges with washi tape. And feel free to add a fancy washi tape design to your car too!

STEP 8: Apply crafter's tape to the back of the circle with the 1 on it and press it firmly to the top of the car at the front.

Place the steering wheel into the opening in the top of the car and hold it in place with a piece of tape on the inside of the paper roll.

STEP 9: Your paper roll car is complete!

STEP 2: Cut the scrap of wrapping paper into a rectangle, just large enough to cover the paper roll. Wrap the paper around the paper roll and tape the ends to hold it in place.

Cut out an opening in the top of the car, about 1 inch (2.5 cm) wide and 2 inches (5 cm) long, rounded at one end. Don't worry if your opening is a little messy, you can cover it with washi tape later.

Using the single hole punch, punch 2 holes about ½ inch (1.3 cm) from the front end of the paper roll, directly across from each other. Then punch 2 holes about ½ inch (1.3 cm) from the back end of the paper roll, directly across from each other.

Candy Box Traffic Lights

LEVEL OF DIFFICULTY 3/5 ✦ PARENTAL SUPERVISION
ASK A GROWN UP TO HELP WITH THE GLUE GUN.

THIS CRAFT IS A GREAT WAY to upcycle empty candy boxes. I don't know about you, but we always seem to have tons of candy in our house. Especially after Halloween and Valentine's Day. I used a mini Smarties box for these traffic lights and the size was perfect!

DON'T YOU THINK sticker rhinestones are the perfect, low-mess craft supply for the lights? You don't need any glue to attach them and they sparkle in the sunlight, just like real lights!

MATERIALS
- 1 Smarties, or similar mini candy, box
- 3 large sticker rhinestones (1 red, 1 yellow and 1 green)
- 1 piece of paper (orange or yellow)
- 1 drinking straw
- 1 piece of construction paper (black)
- 1 plastic bottle lid

TOOLS
- Scissors
- Low-temperature glue gun
- Glue stick
- Single hole punch
- Tape

STEP 1: Push the flaps at the opening of the empty candy box into the box. Wrap the candy box in orange paper, leaving the bottom end open.

STEP 2: Peel off the sticker rhinestones and press them onto the wrapped candy box. Start with the yellow rhinestone in the middle first, then add the red rhinestone above it and the green rhinestone evenly spaced below it.

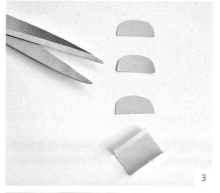

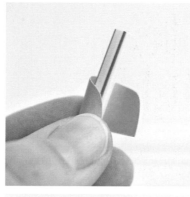

STEP 3: Cut out 3 semicircle shapes from the orange paper. Then cut out an orange paper rectangle to cover the open end at the bottom of the candy box.

STEP 4: Curl each of the semicircles around the drinking straw to give them a slight curve.

STEP 5: Add 3 small dots of hot glue onto the flat edge of one of the curved semicircle pieces—one at each end, and one in the middle. Then press it to the top edge of one of the rhinestones. Repeat for the other 2 rhinestones.

STEP 6: Cut out a rectangle of black construction paper the same width as the drinking straw. Tape the drinking straw to the edge of the rectangle. Apply glue to the entire inside surface of the construction paper using a glue stick. Carefully roll the paper around the straw, pressing down on it as you go to make sure the glue sticks.

STEP 7: Punch a hole in the piece of orange paper that was cut to cover the bottom of the candy box. Slide it onto the straw.

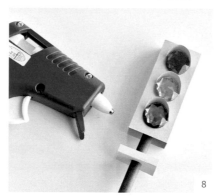

STEP 8: Add a glob of hot glue to the end of the straw, then carefully push it into the candy box, all the way to the end, making sure it ends up in the center. Once the hot glue has dried, slide the orange rectangle into the bottom of the candy box and attach it with a couple small dots of glue from the glue gun.

STEP 9: Squeeze a generous glob of hot glue onto the top of the plastic bottle lid. Press the other end of the straw into the hot glue. Make sure you hold it up straight for at least 20 to 30 seconds while the glue dries.

STEP 10: Your candy box traffic light is complete!

Tissue Box Fire Truck

LEVEL OF DIFFICULTY 3/5 + PARENTAL SUPERVISION NOT REQUIRED.

YOU CAN USE EMPTY TISSUE BOXES to make all sorts of fun vehicles! After you're finished making a fire truck, try making a school bus, an ambulance or even a train. When you use construction paper to give your boxes color instead of painting them, it's quick and easy to use different colors and patterns to make all sorts of low-mess vehicles!

THERE ARE SO MANY DIFFERENT WAYS to make wheels for your vehicles. You can use cardboard, plastic lids, bottle caps, jar lids or even coasters. If you don't want to use craft foam, take a look in the recycling bin and see what you can find!

MATERIALS

- 4 pieces of construction paper (2 red, 1 white and 1 black)
- 1 tissue box
- 1 foam cup
- 1 piece of black craft foam
- 4 medium sticker rhinestones (2 red, 2 white)
- 2 large sticker rhinestones (yellow)

TOOLS

- Scissors
- Glue stick
- Tape
- Pencil
- Crafter's tape

STEP 1: Cut out 2 rectangles of red construction paper to cover the 2 ends of the tissue box. Apply glue with a glue stick and press them onto the tissue box. Add some extra tape to the edges to keep them in place.

STEP 2: Wrap the rest of the tissue box with red construction paper, making sure you apply glue from the glue stick to the paper before you attach it to the box. Hold the edges in place with some tape.

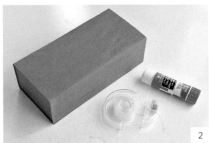

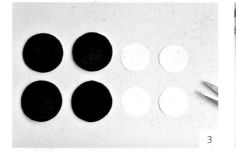

3

4

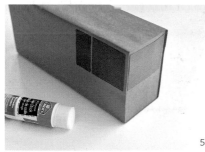

5

6

7

8

STEP 6: Cut out another rectangle of black construction paper, about 3 inches (7.5 cm) wide and 2 inches (5 cm) long.

Make a fold about ½ inch (1.3 cm) from the long edge. Make another fold ½ inch (1.3 cm) from the first fold, then make a third fold ½ inch (1.3 cm) from the second fold to make a triangle shape.

Apply glue to the inside edge of the construction paper with a glue stick, then press down the edge to hold it in place.

STEP 7: Peel off the red and white sticker rhinestones and carefully press them onto the black paper triangle piece to make the fire truck's flashing lights. Attach the triangle piece to the top of the tissue box using crafter's tape, making sure the lights point towards the front.

Cut out long, thin strips of white construction paper. Next, cut and glue these strips onto your fire truck with a glue stick to make all the details on the truck. Try adding a ladder, stripes, bumper, numbers, fire hose, etc.

STEP 8: Peel off the yellow sticker rhinestones and press them to the front of the fire truck to make the fire truck's headlights.

STEP 9: Apply crafter's tape to the back of the wheels (only on the top half), then press them onto the fire truck so the top half of the wheel is on the tissue box and the bottom half of the wheel extends over the edge.

STEP 10: Your tissue box fire truck is complete!

9

STEP 3: With a sharp pencil, trace around the larger edge of a foam cup onto the black foam to make 4 circles.

Trace around the smaller edge of the foam cup onto the white construction paper to make 4 circles.

Cut out each of the circles so you end up with 4 black circles and 4 smaller white circles.

STEP 4: Apply crafter's tape to one side of the white circles, then press them onto the center of the black foam circles.

STEP 5: Cut out rectangles of black construction paper to make the windows on the fire truck. Apply glue to the back of the rectangles with a glue stick and attach them to the front and sides of the tissue box.

10

Shampoo Bottle Gas Station

LEVEL OF DIFFICULTY 3/5 ✦ PARENTAL SUPERVISION
ASK A GROWN UP TO HELP WITH THE GLUE GUN.

DONT FORGET ABOUT used plastic bottles when you're making your crafts! These travel sized shampoo bottles make fantastic little gas pumps! I used red electrical tape (from the dollar store, of course) to cover them, and they look just like vintage gas pumps.

COLORED ELECTRICAL TAPE is a great way to add color to oddly shaped items like plastic bottles. You can completely hide the bottle underneath and transform it into a bright and bold solid color—with no paint and no mess!

STEP 1: Press the end of the red electrical tape onto the bottom of the mini shampoo bottle. Then stretch the tape up towards the top of the bottle, pressing down any bubbles in the tape as you go. Stretch the tape over the top and back down to the bottom. Shift the tape over slightly each time you go around the bottle until the entire bottle is covered.

STEP 2: Cut out a small circle shape (try tracing around the edge of the electrical tape to make the circle). Make sure you leave a small tab at the bottom of the circle so you can attach it to your gas pump later.

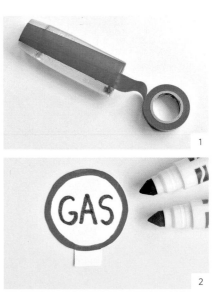

3

4

5

6

7

8

9

STEP 4: Peel off the backing from the sparkly star sticker and press it onto the front of the shampoo bottle, underneath the white rectangle.

Bend the tab at the bottom of the "GAS" circle backwards and apply crafter's tape to the bottom of the tab. Press it onto the middle of the top of the shampoo bottle.

STEP 5: Roll the end of the black pipe cleaner into a small tight spiral. Bend the spiral downwards at a right angle, right where the spiral ends.

STEP 6: On the other end of the black pipe cleaner, cross the end over the pipe cleaner to make a medium sized loop.

STEP 7: Take the long end of the pipe cleaner and wrap it around the loop and bend it straight upwards.

STEP 8: Wind it around the pipe cleaner loop about 3 times. Bend it into the shape of a gas pump nozzle.

STEP 9: Add a small loop in the long part of the pipe cleaner between the nozzle and the spiral.

Using a glue gun, attach the spiral part of the black pipe cleaner near the bottom of the side of the shampoo bottle.

Add a small dot of glue onto the tip of the pipe cleaner nozzle and attach it to the side of the shampoo bottle near the top.

Your shampoo bottle gas station is complete!

Color around the outer edge of the circle with the red washable marker. Then write "GAS" in the middle of the circle with the black washable marker.

STEP 3: Use the label maker to print out "00.00 00.00 TOTAL" in small letters. Cut out the "00.00"s and the "TOTAL" into 3 long thin rectangles, trying to make each one the same width.

Cut out a small rectangle shape from the thick white paper, so that it fits the pieces printed from the label maker.

Peel off the backing from each label and attach the words and numbers to the small white rectangle. Then attach the white rectangle to the front of the shampoo bottle using crafter's tape.

HINT: If you don't have a label maker at home, ask a grown up to print out the numbers from the computer. Then cut them out and tape them onto your gas pump. And if you don't have a way to print things out, simply write out the numbers on black construction paper with a white pencil crayon.

2D Wheelie Police Cars

LEVEL OF DIFFICULTY 2/5 ✦ PARENTAL SUPERVISION NOT REQUIRED.

THIS IS SUCH A SIMPLE CRAFT and the wheels actually spin! You know those little apple sauce snack pouches? Save their caps and you instantly have absolutely amazing wheels for your craft projects!

REMEMBER TO KEEP AN EYE OUT for self-adhesive materials that you can use for your low-mess craft projects. I used white sticker labels for the car's windows and a foam sticker for the star. You could even use red electrical tape for the red light. With a little creativity, sometimes you can completely skip the glue all together!

MATERIALS
- 1 piece of thick paper (blue)
- 1 self adhesive label (white)
- 1 scrap of paper (red)
- 1 milkshake straw (they're wider than a regular straw)
- 2 sparkly foam star stickers
- 4 apple sauce pouch lids

TOOLS
- Scissors
- Pencil
- Single hole punch
- Glue stick

STEP 1: Fold the thick blue paper in half. Then cut along the fold to make 2 rectangles. As long as your paper was 8.5 inches x 11 inches (21.5 x 28 cm) standard letter size, you will only need one of these rectangles.

STEP 2: Fold the rectangle in half. Draw a car shape on the paper so that the top of the car is on the fold in the paper.

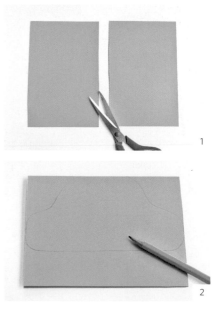

STEP 4: Cut the milkshake straw into 2 pieces, both about 1½ inches (3.8 cm) long.

STEP 5: Using the outer edge of the milkshake straw, trace 2 circles onto the bottom edge of the car where the wheels will go.

Use the single hole punch to cut out the holes for these circles. If you have a regular sized single hole punch, you'll need to punch several times, slowly going around the edge of each traced circle to make the hole large enough for the straw to fit through.

STEP 6: Fold the red rectangle in half. Attach it to the top of the car using a glue stick.

Peel the backing off from the white label rectangles and attach them in the top part of the car to make the windows.

Peel the backing off from the sparkly star sticker and attach it in the middle of the car, beneath the windows.

STEP 7: Press the end of each straw piece into the opening of the apple sauce pouch lids. Push them all the way in until they're snug at the end of the lid.

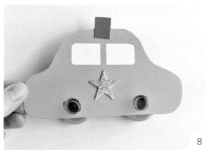

STEP 8: Push the straws through the holes in the bottom of the car. The holes should be big enough that the wheels spin freely.

STEP 9: Press the other 2 apple sauce pouch lids onto the milkshake straws, making sure you push firmly to make them snug. If your lids are too big for the straws, add some glue inside the opening in the lid before you insert the straw.

STEP 10: Your 2D wheelie police car is complete!

HINT: Don't limit yourself to police cars—you can make all sorts of fun and easy vehicles using this method such as cars, trucks, vans or even school buses. All you have to do is change the shape of the car slightly, use a different paper color, and you'll have a completely new vehicle to add to your fleet.

STEP 3: Cut out the car shape.

Cut out a strip of the white label, about ¾ inch (1.9 cm) wide. Cut the corners into a curve, then cut the strip in half.

Cut out a long skinny rectangle from the red paper, about a ½ inch (1.3 cm) wide and 1½ inches (3.8 cm) long.

Simple Paper Street Signs

LEVEL OF DIFFICULTY 3/5 ✦ PARENTAL SUPERVISION
ASK A GROWN UP TO HELP WITH THE GLUE GUN..

MATERIALS
- 6 pieces of thick paper (green, black, blue, white, yellow and red)
- White chalk marker
- 3 wooden skewers
- 5 mini wooden blocks (available at the craft store or dollar store)

TOOLS
- Scissors
- Crafter's tape
- Low-temperature glue gun

STREET SIGNS ARE SO SIMPLE TO MAKE. Once you've made one, all the different sign types are pretty much exactly the same concept. They just use slightly different shapes and colors—which means you can keep making different signs without pulling out more materials!

DON'T WORRY ONE BIT if you don't have everything. You can use craft sticks or straws to hold up your signs if you don't have wooden skewers. And you can use bottle caps, or small squares cut from a cardboard box instead of using small wooden blocks. Remember to cut your paper over the top of a large placemat or baking sheet to make it easy to collect those tiny paper scraps when you're done!

STEP 1: Cut out a black square and a yellow square, both about 1½ inches (3.8 cm) wide. Trim the yellow square to make it slightly smaller than the black square. Cut out 2 thin black rectangles and a small black triangle.

STEP 2: Apply crafter's tape to one side of the yellow square and attach it to the middle of the black square. Partially turn the square to make it a diamond, with the points at the top and bottom.

Use crafter's tape to attach the thin rectangles as a cross to the middle of the yellow square. Then use crafter's tape to attach the black triangle to the top of the cross.

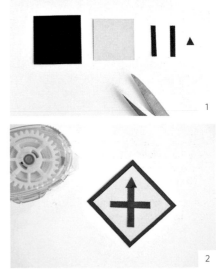

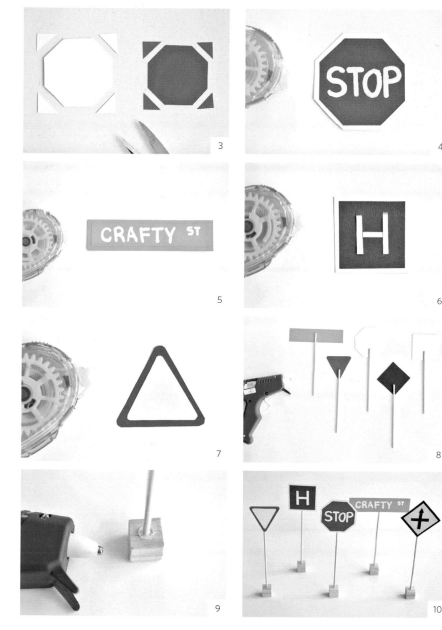

STEP 5: Cut out 2 green rectangles, about 1 inch (2.5 cm) wide and 2½ inches (6.5 cm) long. Trim one of the rectangles to make it slightly smaller than the other rectangle.

Apply crafter's tape to one side of the smaller green rectangle and attach it to the middle of the larger green rectangle.

Use a white chalk marker to write "CRAFTY ST" in the middle of the smaller rectangle. You can name your street whatever you like! If it's a longer word, cut out a longer rectangle to make it fit.

STEP 6: Cut out a white square and a blue square, both about 1.5 inches (3.8 cm) wide. Trim the blue square to make it slightly smaller than the white square.

Cut out 3 thin white rectangles, all the same size. Then cut one of the thin rectangles in half.

Apply crafter's tape to one side of the blue square and attach it to the middle of the white square. Use crafter's tape to attach the thin rectangles to the middle of the blue square in an "H" shape.

STEP 7: Cut out a red triangle and a white triangle, so that each edge is about 1.5 inches (3.8 cm) long. Trim the white triangle to make it slightly smaller than the red triangle. Cut each corner of each triangle to make them slightly rounded.

Apply crafter's tape to one side of the white triangle and attach it to the middle of the red triangle.

STEP 8: Cut off the pointy end of each wooden skewer then cut each skewer in half. If your scissors won't cut through the skewer, use them to make a deep indent all the way around the skewer, then snap the skewer at the indent.

Attach the skewers to the back of each street sign using a glue gun.

STEP 9: Squeeze a glob of glue from the glue gun onto the top of a mini wooden block. Press the end of the skewer into the glob of glue, making sure you hold the sign up straight for about 20 to 30 seconds until the hot glue dries. Repeat for the other 4 street signs.

STEP 10: Your simple paper street signs are complete!

STEP 3: Cut out a white square and a red square, both about 1½ inches (3.8 cm) wide. Trim the red square to make it slightly smaller than the white square.

Cut the corners off each of the squares to shape them into an octagon.

STEP 4: Apply crafter's tape to one side of the red octagon and attach it to the middle of the white octagon.

Use a white chalk marker to write "STOP" in the middle of the red octagon.

Poster Board Road Track

LEVEL OF DIFFICULTY 3/5 + PARENTAL SUPERVISION NOT REQUIRED.

MATERIALS
- 1 piece of poster board (green)
- Duct tape (black)
- White roll-on correction tape
- 1 piece of paper (blue)

TOOLS
- Pencil
- Ruler
- Scissors
- Washable marker (blue)

THERE ARE SO MANY FUN AND INEXPENSIVE WAYS to create a road track! Use these instructions as a starting point, but feel free to make your track with whatever materials you have at home. You only need a few materials and there's barely any scraps, so cleanup is easy!

IF YOU DONT HAVE BLACK DUCT TAPE, cut out strips of black construction paper and use a glue stick to attach them. You could even draw the roads right onto the poster board with black marker. I left my trees, grass and pond pieces loose so my kids could move them around, but if you'd prefer to glue yours down, it's completely up to you! Be creative and see what you can come up with.

STEP 1: Draw a line across the long edge of the poster board, exactly 2 inches (5 cm) from the edge. Cut across the line so you have a 2 inch (5 cm) strip of paper.

STEP 2: Cut different sizes of rectangles from the strip of paper. Cut the longer rectangles into the shape of trees with a short trunk.

Cut a fringe into the smaller rectangles to make some tall grass. Bend back the uncut edge of the long grass pieces so they can stand on their own. Next, bend back the trunk of each tree so they can stand on their own.

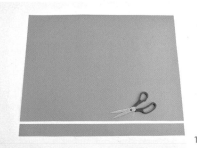

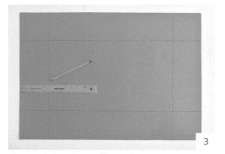

3

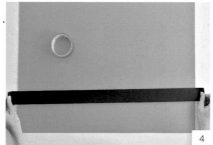

4

5

6

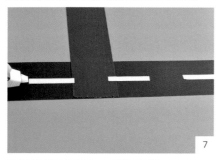

7

8

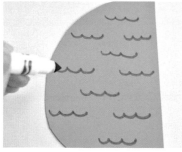

9

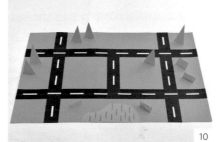

10

STEP 3: Using a ruler, draw 4 lines, each line exactly 4½ inches (11.5 cm) from each edge of the poster board. It's okay if these lines aren't perfect. They're just meant to guide you so the roads are straight. They'll be hidden later by the duct tape.

STEP 4: Cut a piece of duct tape about 2 inches (5 cm) longer than the poster board. Stretch it over one of the lines on the poster board, then slowly and carefully lower it onto the poster board. Duct tape is much stickier than regular tape, so be extra careful to make sure you don't accidentally let the tape touch the poster board before you're ready.

STEP 5: Fold the extra duct tape at each end neatly over the edge and under the poster board.

STEP 6: Repeat Step 4 and Step 5 for the other 3 lines drawn on the poster board.

Cut a shorter piece of duct tape, then carefully add it in the middle to connect 2 of the roads.

STEP 7: Apply long white lines down the middle of the duct tape using white correction tape.

STEP 8: Cut a pond shape from the blue piece of paper.

STEP 9: Draw some wave shapes onto the pond using the blue washable marker.

STEP 10: Set your trees, tall grass and pond onto your road track. Your poster board road track is complete!

HINT: If you can't find any white correction tape for the lines in the road you can also use white self-adhesive labels, cut into thin strips. Just peel off the backing and they'll stick right to the tape.

Snowy Mountain Cardboard Tunnel

LEVEL OF DIFFICULTY 5/5 ✦ PARENTAL SUPERVISION—ASK A GROWN UP TO HELP WITH THE GLUE GUN AND WITH CUTTING THE CARDBOARD.

THIS CARDBOARD TUNNEL goes perfectly with the Poster Board Road Track we made earlier in this chapter (page 118). Make the roads line up and your cars can drive right over the mountain. I used a tri-fold display board to make this tunnel (the kind you would use for a science fair project), mostly because it's white on one side, and white is the perfect color for a snowy mountain. But you can use any old cardboard box.

SOMETIMES BIG PROJECTS are easier to clean up than small projects. It's much easier to collect big cardboard scraps than it is to gather small pieces!

MATERIALS
- Tri-fold display board (or a large cardboard box)
- 1 piece of paper (white)
- Duct tape (black)
- White roll on correction tape
- White chalk marker

TOOLS
- Pencil
- Ruler
- Scissors
- Single hole punch
- Glue stick
- Low-temperature glue gun

STEP 1: With a pencil, draw a pointy mountain shape on the cardboard. Make sure you include an opening at the bottom to make a tunnel. Use a ruler to help make straight lines.

STEP 2: Cut out the mountain, then trace its shape onto another piece of cardboard and cut out a second, identical mountain. Cut out a long rectangle, about 5 inches (12.5 cm) wide. The length will depend on the size of your mountains.

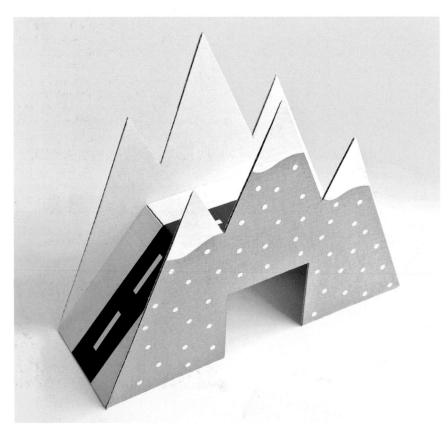

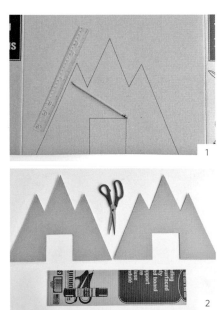

STEP 3: Trace the tips of each mountain point onto white paper. Cut out 6 triangles with a curved bottom so each mountain point can have a snowy peak.

STEP 4: Use a white chalk marker to add snow to your mountain. The more dots you add, the snowier the mountain will look! Repeat for the second mountain piece.

STEP 5: Apply glue to the back of the white triangles using a glue stick and attach them to each of the 3 mountain peaks.

STEP 6: Starting with one end at the bottom corner of the mountain, bend the long rectangle up over the tunnel and back down towards the opposite corner of the mountain. Trim the rectangle if it's too long.

Hold the rectangular piece in place and squeeze glue from the glue gun along the entire inside edge to hold it in place.

STEP 7: Flip the mountain over onto the other mountain piece and line up the corners. Squeeze glue from the glue gun along the entire inside edge to hold it in place. Flip over the mountain to stand it upright.

STEP 8: Cut a piece of black duct tape so that it's slightly longer than the top of your mountain. Stretch the piece of duct tape over the mountain and slowly lower it into place in the middle.

Fold the extra duct tape at each end neatly over the edge and under the cardboard.

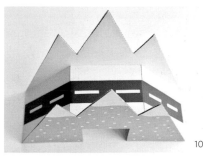

STEP 9: Apply long white lines down the middle of the duct tape using white correction tape.

STEP 10: Your snowy mountain cardboard tunnel is complete!

> **HINT:** You don't even need to cut your cardboard box into a mountain shape if you're in a hurry. You can glue pieces of paper to the side of a shoe box in the shape of a mountain for a quick and simple alternative.

Chapter 7

Exploring OUTER SPACE

Build yourself a sleek little rocket ship (page 124) and blast off into outer space! Make some new alien friends (page 128), then send the astronauts (page 126) on a special mission to collect the sparkliest space rocks (page 134) they can find. The view of the planets and stars is out of this world!

⇒ LOW-MESS TIP: COME UP WITH A PLAN TO KEEP THINGS CLEAN ⇐

Just because a material has a chance of getting messy (like glue, paint, glitter, etc.), doesn't mean you have to avoid it completely. It just means you have to come up with a plan to keep any potential mess contained. Sometimes it's as simple as covering the kitchen table with an inexpensive plastic tablecloth from the dollar store or making your craft on top of an aluminum foil lined baking sheet (you'll probably want to do both of those things when you're making the planet sun catchers in this chapter).

Other times it's all about the location you choose. Using paint while sitting on the living room rug is never a good idea! But using small amounts of the washable paint used in the glittering space rocks at the kitchen counter is a much better plan! You'll be close to the kitchen sink and you'll have easy access to dishcloths and paper towels if you need them. A little planning goes a long way!

Paper Roll Rocket Ship (page 124), Peg Doll Astronauts (page 126), Plastic Bottle Alien (page 128),
Paper Plate Flying Saucer (page 130), Planet Sun Catchers (page 132), Glittering Space Rocks (page 134),
Upcycled CD Saturn Model (page 136), Sparkly Star Mobile (page 138)

Paper Roll Rocket Ship

LEVEL OF DIFFICULTY 3/5 ✦ PARENTAL SUPERVISION NOT REQUIRED.

THIS PAPER ROLL ROCKET SHIP is so simple to make and so much fun to play with! My son was so excited to make rocket sounds and fly his rocket through the air. The tissue paper flutters and looks so much like real flames when it's moving.

I USED LITTLE WHITE CIRCLE STICKERS for the windows. They're the kind you get from the office supply store (or the stationary section of many other stores). They're self-adhesive and you don't have to trace or cut them out, which means fewer scraps and fewer things to put away. You can easily add as many (or as few) windows as you like!

MATERIALS
- 3 pieces of paper (red, blue and green)
- 1 toilet paper roll
- 3 circle stickers (white)
- Small round bowl or plate (about 4½" [11.4 cm] across)
- 1 piece of tissue paper (yellow)

TOOLS
- Scissors
- Tape
- Pencil
- White glue

STEP 1: Cut out a rectangle of green paper, just large enough to cover the toilet paper roll. Tape one end of the paper to the toilet paper roll, making sure the edges line up.

Roll the paper around the toilet paper roll to completely cover it. Apply a long strip of tape to the end to keep it in place.

STEP 2: Cut out 3 right angle triangles from the blue paper. Trim ⅛ inch (0.3 cm) from the top point of each triangle so each one has a short flat edge on the top.

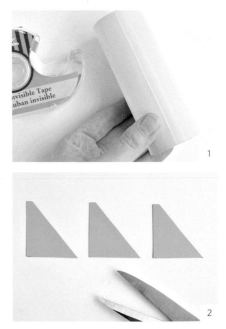

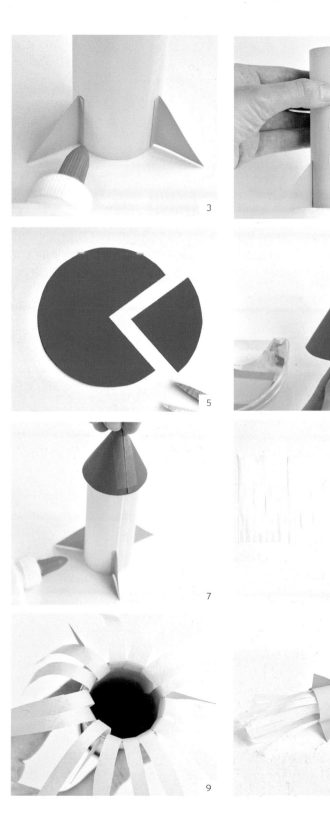

STEP 3: Fold in the edge of each triangle (the edge with the flat point on top) by about ⅛ inch (0.3 cm).

Squeeze a thin line of white glue onto the ⅛ inch (0.3 cm) fold on the triangle and attach it to the paper roll near the bottom edge. Repeat for each triangle, spacing them evenly around the paper roll.

STEP 4: Peel off the white circle stickers and press them onto the front of the paper roll to make the rocket ship's windows.

STEP 5: Trace around the edge of the round bowl with a pencil to make a circle shape.

Cut out the circle shape. Next, cut out a quarter from the circle as if you were cutting out a piece of pie.

STEP 6: Roll the larger circle piece into a cone so that the bottom of the cone is just larger than the end of the paper roll. Add a piece of tape to the edge on the outside and inside of the cone to hold it together.

STEP 7: Squeeze a line of white glue around the top edge of the paper roll. Line up the taped edge of the cone so it's directly above the taped edge of the paper roll. Press the cone down onto the white glue. Allow the glue to dry.

STEP 8: Cut out 4 rectangles of tissue paper, about 2 inches (5 cm) wide by 5 inches (12.5 cm) long. Cut a fringe into the short edge of each of the rectangles.

STEP 9: Slide one of the pieces of tissue paper into the paper roll and hold it in place with a piece of tape. Continue adding the tissue paper pieces to the inside of the paper roll and taping them in place until you've gone around the entire inside edge of the paper roll.

STEP 10: Your paper roll rocket ship is complete!

Peg Doll Astronauts

LEVEL OF DIFFICULTY 3/5 ✦ PARENTAL SUPERVISION NOT REQUIRED.

THESE PEG DOLL ASTRONAUTS are so cute and so simple to make! You can usually find wooden peg dolls at the craft store, but if you have trouble finding them, try checking online. I suggest searching for "wooden peg dolls" on Amazon.com or Etsy.com to find a great assortment of affordable options.

KEEP THE PAINTING MESS TO A MINIMUM by only squeezing out small amounts of paint, and only add more as you need it. It doesn't take much paint to cover the peg dolls, and the less paint you use, the easier it is to keep your painting station tidy. Then you can let your peg doll dry on the plate and when everything is dry, toss the plate in the trash and the mess is gone!

MATERIALS
- Wooden peg dolls
- Paint (white)
- Paint pen (gold)
- Disposable plate

TOOLS
- White glue
- Washable marker (black)
- Masking tape
- Scissors
- Paint brush

STEP 1: Squeeze a small glob of white glue onto the peg doll where you plan to draw the face. Use your finger to spread the glue into an even layer.

Allow the glue to dry. This will help keep the ink from the marker from bleeding. If you add a very thin layer of glue it should dry in less than 10 minutes.

STEP 2: Draw the astronaut's face onto the area with the dry white glue.

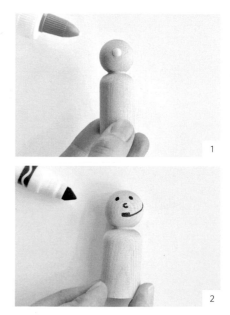

STEP 3: Cut out a small oval shape from the masking tape. Make sure the oval is large enough to cover the astronaut's entire face.

STEP 4: Press the oval shaped piece of tape onto the astronaut's face. Use your thumb nail to push out any bubbles in the masking tape and to make sure the edge is sealed tightly the entire way around.

STEP 5: Squeeze a small amount of white paint onto the disposable plate. Holding the peg doll between your thumb and pointer finger, paint the entire peg doll with white paint.

Stand up the peg doll on the paper plate to dry. Add a second coat of paint.

STEP 6: When the paint is completely dry, carefully peel off the masking tape oval from the face.

STEP 7: Use a gold paint pen to draw circles on either side of the peg doll's head, about where the ears would be. Then draw circles and a rectangle down the front of the peg doll for the space suit controls. Allow the gold paint to dry.

STEP 8: Your peg doll astronaut is complete!

> HINT: Don't forget to cover your work surface with a plastic table cloth or newspaper to protect it from the paint!

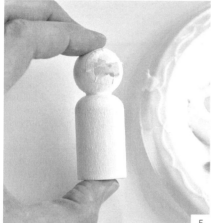

Plastic Bottle
⌒ Alien ⌒

LEVEL OF DIFFICULTY 2/5 ✦ PARENTAL SUPERVISION
ASK A GROWN UP TO HELP WITH THE GLUE GUN.

DON'T YOU THINK these green plastic Perrier bottles make perfect little aliens? You can find lots of ways to paint a plastic bottle online, but why bother pulling out all those messy painting supplies when you can find plastic bottles in the exact color you need?!

LOTS OF DIFFERENT SODAS come in green bottles, or you can use a lemon juice bottle, or even a shampoo bottle. Check out the recycling bin to see if you have anything green to use for your alien.

STEP 1: Peel the label off the green plastic bottle. Center a green pipe cleaner under the neck of the bottle.

STEP 2: Wrap the pipe cleaner around the neck and twist it twice to hold it in place. Bend each of the ends straight upwards. Turn the bottle so the twisted pipe cleaner is at the back.

3

5

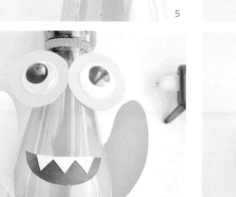

7

6

STEP 3: Attach the pom poms to each end of the pipe cleaner using a glue gun.

STEP 4: Trace around the edge of a glue stick on the green paper to make 2 circle shapes, then cut them out.

Draw 2 rounded arm shapes on the green paper and cut them out.

STEP 5: Apply crafter's tape to the back of the googly eyes and press each one onto the middle of each green circle.

Apply crafter's tape to the back of the green circles, covering a little less than one half of the back with tape (since part of the eyes will hang off the side). Press the eyes onto the bottle.

STEP 6: Cut out a black mouth piece and some jagged white teeth from the black and white paper.

Apply glue to the back of the white teeth with a glue stick and press them onto the black mouth so the top edges line up.

Apply crafter's tape to the back of the mouth and press it firmly in place onto the bottle.

STEP 7: Attach the green paper arms to the sides of the bottle using a glue gun. Squeeze the glue behind the arms so you can't see it from the front.

STEP 8: Your plastic bottle alien is complete!

8

Paper Plate Flying Saucer

LEVEL OF DIFFICULTY 1/5 ✦ PARENTAL SUPERVISION NOT REQUIRED.

THE GREAT THING ABOUT ALIENS is that you can make them whatever shape you want! If you'd like your alien to be a big blob, that totally works! If you want yours to have 8 arms, even better! Add googly eyes and a smile and you can pretty much turn any shape into an alien.

DECORATING YOUR CRAFTS with stickers is such a fun and low-mess way to make your projects look awesome! Don't limit yourself to star stickers—see what other stickers you have in your collection and be creative with the patterns. Don't forget to add something to the bottom too!

MATERIALS
- 1 clear plastic cup
- 1 paper dessert plate
- Sparkly star stickers
- 1 piece of polka dot scrapbook paper
- 2 small googly eyes

TOOLS
- Pencil
- Scissors
- Tape
- White glue
- Washable marker (red)

STEP 1: Place the plastic cup with the open side down onto the middle of the paper plate. Trace around the edge of the plastic cup with a pencil.

STEP 2: Cut out the circle shape from the paper plate so that the hole is a little bit smaller than the pencil line you drew.

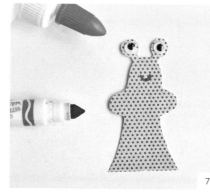

STEP 3: Slide the plastic cup through the hole in the paper plate.

STEP 4: Tape the edges of the plastic cup to the paper plate to hold it in place.

STEP 5: Add sparkly star stickers to the paper plate to decorate your flying saucer.

STEP 6: Draw a funny looking alien shape onto the back of the scrapbook paper.

STEP 7: Cut out the alien shape. Attach the googly eyes to the shape using white glue and give your alien a happy little smile with a red washable marker.

STEP 8: Cut a piece of tape so that it's longer than the opening in the plastic cup. Place the tape sticky side up and press your alien onto the middle of it.

STEP 9: Carefully slide the alien inside the plastic cup. Press the ends of the tape to each side of the inside of the plastic cup to hold the alien in place. Try to use transparent (clear) tape rather than invisible (translucent) tape.

STEP 10: Your paper plate flying saucer is complete!

Planet Sun Catchers

LEVEL OF DIFFICULTY 2/5 ✦ PARENTAL SUPERVISION NOT REQUIRED.

THE HARDEST PART about these planet sun catchers is waiting for them to dry. It can take a few days for the glue to dry, depending on how thick it is, but it's worth the wait! Once it's dry, all the white parts become clear and all the colored parts become translucent, making them perfect for hanging in the window.

ITS EASY to keep the mess to a minimum with a little bit of planning. Line a baking sheet with paper or aluminum foil and set out all of your supplies on it. Make sure you set the plastic lid in the middle of the tray and only add a little bit of glue and paint at a time. Choose a location that's easy to clean just in case—an inexpensive plastic table cloth on the kitchen table helps keeps everything protected.

MATERIALS
- White glue
- Round plastic lid (from a yogurt or sour cream container)
- Paint (assorted colors)
- Toothpick
- Thread
- Suction cup hook

TOOLS
- Scissors

STEP 1: Pour white glue into the middle of the plastic lid. Start with a small amount of glue. You don't want the glue to overflow.

STEP 2: Tilt the lid so that the glue covers the entire inside of the lid. Add more glue if you need to.

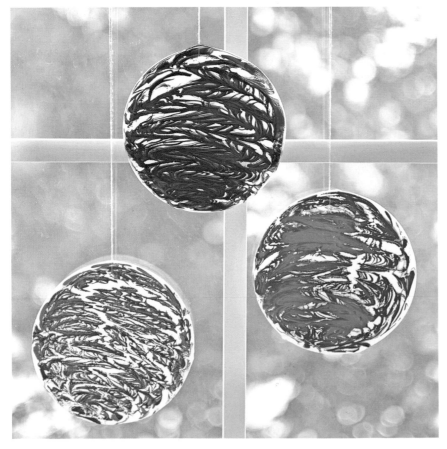

1

2

STEP 3: Squeeze the paint onto the glue. Try to make lines that go from one side of the lid to the other. It's okay if it's not perfect.

STEP 4: Squeeze a second color onto the glue, going back and forth from the top of the lid to the bottom.

STEP 5: Drag the toothpick in straight lines through the paint and glue so that the lines go in the opposite direction of the paint lines. So if your paint lines are going left to right, drag the toothpick up and down from one side of the lid to the other.

STEP 6: Rotate the lid by about a quarter turn. Drag the toothpick left and right through the paint and glue again, this time curving the line up towards the top as you go to make it look like the planet is round.

STEP 7: Set the lids in a safe place and allow the glue to dry for 2 to 4 days.

After about 2 days, carefully bend back the edge of the lid and peel up a small portion of the glue. If the glue doesn't pull out of the lid easily, the glue isn't dry yet. Wait a day and check again.

When the glue is fully dry, carefully peel it off from the plastic lid.

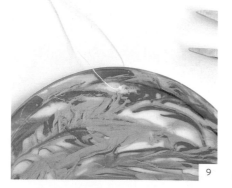

STEP 8: Poke a hole near the top of your planet using a toothpick.

STEP 9: Cut a piece of thread about 12 inches (30.5 cm) long and push the end through the hole in the planet. Tie the 2 ends of the thread together in a knot. Hang your planets on the window from suction cup hooks.

STEP 10: Your planet sun catchers are complete!

Glittering Space Rocks

LEVEL OF DIFFICULTY 3/5 ✦ PARENTAL SUPERVISION NOT REQUIRED.

YOU KNOW THOSE SMALL ROCKS that travel behind a large comet or asteroid? What do you think it would be like to hold one? Would they have little fragments of metal that glimmer in the sunlight? With this simple air-dry clay recipe you can mold your own space rocks to be any size you like. You could even poke small holes in them with toothpicks to make little craters.

WHEN YOU'RE USING SUPPLIES that can potentially be messy, make sure you come up with a clean up plan before you start. Choose a safe place that's easy to clean— this is a great project for the kitchen or bathroom counter since counters are easy to wipe down and you won't have to go far to clean your hands. Just make sure you use washable tempera paint, and cleaning up will be easy!

STEP 1: Combine the baking soda, black paint and white glue in a mixing bowl.

STEP 2: Gently stir the mixture together. It will be white, gray and crumbly in the beginning.

Keep stirring, pressing the back of the spoon into the side of the bowl until the ingredients are combined and the color is consistent.

1

2

3

4

5A

5B

STEP 3: Pour in a generous amount of glitter.

STEP 4: Stir the dough until the glitter is consistently mixed in throughout.

STEP 5: Mold the dough into rock shapes. I made mine about 1 inch (2.5 cm) wide, but you can make them any size or shape.

Set each of the rocks onto the foil lined baking sheet. Let them dry overnight.

Your glittering space rocks are complete!

Upcycled CD Saturn Model

LEVEL OF DIFFICULTY 3/5 ◆ PARENTAL SUPERVISION
ASK A GROWN UP TO HELP WITH THE GLUE GUN AND WITH CUTTING THE FOAM BALL IN HALF.

THE KEY TO WORKING WITH GLITTER is to make sure you have a plan to keep your work space clean. I find that working on full sheets of construction paper that are then placed inside the lid of a large cardboard box really helps keep the glitter mess to a minimum.

WHEN YOU'RE DONE with the glitter, you can fold up the construction paper with the glitter on it and throw it away. Then carefully take the cardboard lid right outside to the recycling bin. If there's any glitter that managed to get onto the table or floor, use a sticky lint roller to clean it up. Always keep the glitter jar inside the cardboard lid as you're working and any potential glitter mess is safely contained!

STEP 1: Glue the 4 mini wooden blocks together with white glue into a larger flat square to make the base for the model. Set it aside to let the glue dry.

STEP 2: Carefully cut the foam ball in half using a craft knife.

Poke the wooden skewer into the bottom of one of the foam ball halves. Squeeze white glue onto the top of the foam ball. Use a paint brush to spread the white glue into an even layer over the entire top of the foam ball.

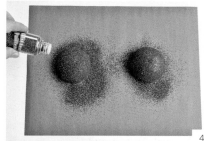

STEP 3: Holding the foam ball right over the top of one of the pieces of contsruction paper, carefully sprinkle the red glitter onto the glue to cover the entire surface.

STEP 4: Carefully remove the foam ball from the skewer and set the ball onto the construction paper.

Repeat these steps to add glitter to the second foam ball half.

Add more glitter to the tops, if needed, to make sure the ball is completely covered with glitter.

STEP 5: Place the CD in the middle of the second piece of construction paper. Squeeze white glue around the top of the CD.

Use a paint brush to spread the glue into an even layer, making sure the entire surface of the CD is covered in glue.

Sprinkle gold glitter onto the CD, making sure the entire surface is covered.

STEP 6: Allow the foam ball halves and the CD to dry. It will take at least 3 hours or more, depending on how much glue you used.

Carefully lift up the CD and tap the back of it over top of the construction paper, allowing the extra glitter to fall onto the construction paper. Lift the foam ball halves and tap the back of them to allow the extra red glitter to fall onto the construction paper.

Carefully fold up each sheet of construction paper to keep the glitter inside and throw them away.

STEP 7: Attach the foam ball halves to the top and bottom of the CD using a glue gun.

STEP 8: Squeeze a generous glob of hot glue onto the middle of the wooden block base. Stick the flat end of the wooden skewer into the glue glob, holding it straight up until the hot glue dries.

STEP 9: Tilt the planet slightly and poke the sharp end of the skewer into the bottom of the planet.

STEP 10: Your upcycled CD Saturn model is complete!

Sparkly Star Mobile

LEVEL OF DIFFICULTY 3/5 ⬩ PARENTAL SUPERVISION
ASK A GROWN UP TO HELP WITH THE GLUE GUN.

MATERIALS
* Thread
* 80 sparkly foam star stickers
* 2 wooden skewers

TOOLS
* Scissors
* Low-temperature glue gun

THIS SPARKLY STAR MOBILE is so simple to make! Just sandwich a piece of thread between two stickers, and repeat! The stickers are already shaped how you need them, so there's no scraps to worry about. And since stickers are already sticky, you don't need any glue to hold them on the string! Easy peasy!

WHEN YOU HANG YOUR MOBILE, the stars will twist, turn and sparkle. I used foam star stickers from the craft store, but you can make yours with flat star stickers too. You can even use the gold stars that teachers use.

STEP 1: Cut 8 pieces of thread, about 18 inches (46 cm) long.

Peel off one sparkly star sticker and place it sticky side up on the table. Take the end of one piece of thread and press it onto the sticky side of the star sticker.

STEP 2: Peel off another sparkly star sticker (make sure it's the same size as the first sticker). Line up the points of the star and press it onto the first star, sticky sides together with the thread in between.

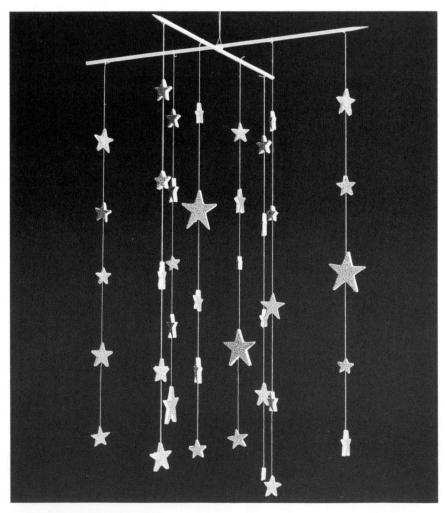

3

4

STEP 3: Peel off another sparkly star sticker and place it sticky side up on the table. Take the thread with the star on the end and place it over the sticky part of the star. Leave about 2 inches (5 cm) of space from the star at the end.

Peel off an identical star, line it up and press it onto the star below, making sure the thread is in between.

STEP 4: Keep pressing stars together with the thread in between, about 2 inches (5 cm) apart until there are 5 stars on the string.

STEP 5: Repeat the process for the next 7 pieces of thread. You'll end up with 8 pieces of thread with 5 stars on each one.

STEP 6: Attach the wooden skewers together in a cross using a glue gun. Set the cross on your work surface.

STEP 7: Tie 2 of the strings to the top of the vertical skewer and pull the strings with the stars to the right side. Tie 2 strings to the bottom of the vertical skewer and pull the strings with the stars to the left side. Make sure they are evenly spaced and be careful not to tangle the threads.

Tie 2 of the strings to the right side of the horizontal skewer and pull the strings with the stars straight down. Tie the last 2 strings to the left side of the horizontal skewer and pull the strings with the stars stright up.

STEP 8: Make sure all of the knots are tight and secure. Add a small dot of glue from the glue gun onto each of the knots to help keep the thread from sliding and to make sure they don't come undone. (White glue works well for this too.) Trim off the extra thread from the knots.

STEP 9: Cut another piece of thread, about 12 inches (30.5 cm) long. Loop it over and around the cross several times where the 2 skewers cross each other. Tie the ends together in a knot.

Carefully lift this thread to raise up your mobile, making sure the threads with the stars don't get tangled.

STEP 10: Your sparkly star mobile is complete!

5

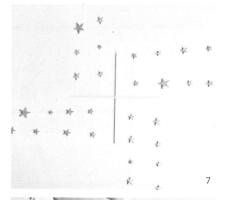

7

8

9

10

Chapter 8

Let's Go CAMPING

Get ready to create your own camping adventure, complete with marshmallows on a campfire (page 142), and colorful tents (page 148) in a forest of paper trees (page 154). You can even build your own picnic table! Make your own bugs and snakes (eek!) and see what mischief your quirky little camping family is going to get into this time!

≽ LOW-MESS TIP: CHOOSE THE LEAST MESSY ADHESIVE POSSIBLE ≼

When you need to stick things together, always choose the least messy adhesive for the job. Use crafter's tape or regular tape instead of glue. Use a glue stick instead of liquid or hot glue. Or skip the glue all together by choosing materials that stick together on their own—like using self-adhesive craft foam or sticker rhinestones. I love that when you're making the Beaded Pipe Cleaner Snakes (page 144) in this chapter, all you have to do is bend the end of the pipe cleaner to hold the beads in place. There's no glue required!

If you don't have to pull out any glue in the first place, that's one less thing to put away! Sometimes glue is the only option, so for those times remember to protect your work surface with a big piece of paper or a large placemat. Then add the glue to your crafts in small amounts. The less glue you add, the fewer drips you'll have and the less sticky your hands will get.

Tissue Paper Campfire (page 142), Beaded Pipe Cleaner Snake (page 144), Craft Stick Camping Family (page 146), Craft Stick Tent (page 148), Paper Roll Frog (page 150), Craft Stick Picnic Table (page 152), Easy Paper Cone Trees (page 154), Simple Quilled Ladybug (page 156)

Tissue Paper Campfire

LEVEL OF DIFFICULTY 3/5 ⟡ PARENTAL SUPERVISION
ASK A GROWN UP TO HELP WITH THE GLUE GUN.

NO CAMPING SITE IS COMPLETE without a fire to roast marshmallows over. And what a fun little fire this is! The battery operated tea light flickers through the tissue paper. Turn off the lights and take a look for yourself! Don't forget to make a pom pom marshmallow or 2 to roast over your campfire.

TISSUE PAPER IS AN AWESOME LOW-MESS CRAFT MATERIAL to use for a pretend fire! You only need a square of each color, and you'll be using the entire sheet of construction paper so, there's no scraps to worry about for this one. What's the best way to make cleaning up easy? Use up all the supplies you pull out so you have less to put away!

MATERIALS
- 1 piece of construction paper (brown)
- 1 wooden skewer
- 3 pieces of tissue paper (red, orange and yellow)
- 1 battery operated tea light
- 1 small elastic
- 1 small pom pom (white)
- 1 toothpick

TOOLS
- Scissors
- Crafter's tape
- Low-temperature glue gun

STEP 1: Cut the construction paper into 5 strips, about 2 inches (5 cm) wide each.

Wrap the end of one of the construction paper strips around the wooden skewer. Roll the paper tightly around itself and the skewer until you reach the end of the paper.

STEP 2: Slide the rolled paper off the skewer and let the spiral open up a little bit. Apply crafter's tape to the inside edge and press the edge down to hold it together.

Repeat for the other 4 strips of construction paper to make 5 logs for your campfire.

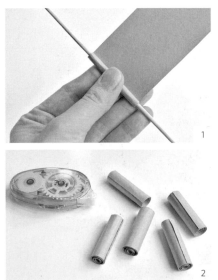

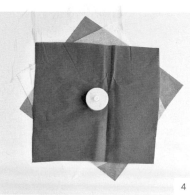

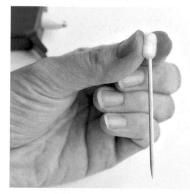

3

4

5

6

7

8

9

10

STEP 3: Cut out 3 squares of tissue paper (1 red, 1 orange and 1 yellow), about 8 x 8 inches (20.3 x 20.3 cm).

STEP 4: Lay the orange, yellow and red squares of tissue paper on top of each other, each one turned slightly so the corners don't line up

Place the battery operated tea light into the middle of the squares of tissue paper.

STEP 5: Wrap all 3 layers of tissue paper up and around the tea light. Pinch the tissue paper tightly at the top of the tea light and stretch a small elastic over top to hold it in place.

STEP 6: Angle the construction paper logs so one end rests on the top edge of the tea light. Glue it in place with a glue gun. Repeat for the other 4 logs, evenly spacing them around the tea light.

STEP 7: Separate each layer of tissue paper to shape the flame of your campfire.

STEP 8: Use your finger nail to find the on/off switch at the bottom of the tea light. Carefully tear a little hole in the tissue paper to make it easier to turn the tea light on and off.

STEP 9: Attach the white pom pom to the end of the toothpick with a glue gun. Roll the pom pom between your fingers to flatten it into a marshmallow shape.

STEP 10: Your tissue paper campfire is complete!

Beaded Pipe Cleaner Snake

LEVEL OF DIFFICULTY 1/5 ✦ PARENTAL SUPERVISION NOT REQUIRED.

MATERIALS
- 1 pipe cleaner
- Plastic pony beads (approximately 35 of them)
- 2 small googly eyes

TOOLS
- Crafter's tape

THESE SLITHERY SNAKES are so simple to make, but they look awesome! You can make yours in any color you like. Make a pattern with your beads, or put them on randomly—It's completely up to you. Don't forget to bend the little guy into a curvy snake shape when you're done!

THIS IS A FANTASTIC LOW-MESS ACTIVITY for all ages and it's a great craft to make in groups or at birthday parties. I love pipe cleaner crafts where bending the pipe cleaner does the job of holding everything in place. You only need a few craft supplies, you don't need any glue and you don't need to cut anything, so there are no scraps!

STEP 1: Curl one end of the pipe cleaner into an oval shaped spiral, going around the spiral 2 or 3 times. Pinch the end of the spiral and shape it into the snake's head.

STEP 2: Slide pony beads onto the pipe cleaner. Mix up the colors, or make a perfect pattern. It's up to you!

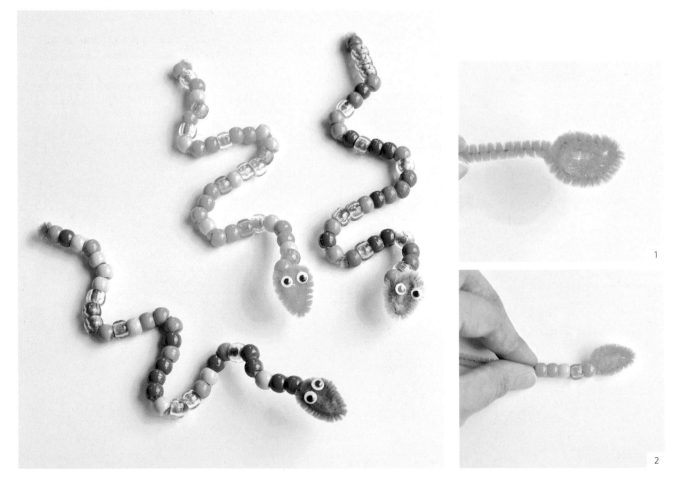

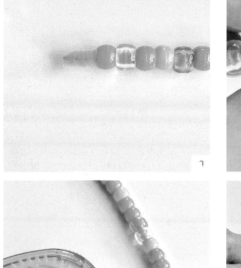

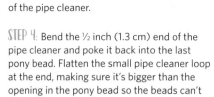

STEP 3: Continue adding pony beads until there is only ½ inch (1.3 cm) left from the end of the pipe cleaner.

STEP 4: Bend the ½ inch (1.3 cm) end of the pipe cleaner and poke it back into the last pony bead. Flatten the small pipe cleaner loop at the end, making sure it's bigger than the opening in the pony bead so the beads can't slide off.

If the beads still slip over the loop, remove a bead, and try bending the pipe cleaner again until the beads are snug and don't slip off the end.

STEP 5: Apply crafter's tape to the back of the googly eyes and press them onto the snake's face.

STEP 6: Bend the beaded pipe cleaner body back and forth to give the snake a curvy "S" shape.

STEP 7: Your beaded pipe cleaner snake is complete!

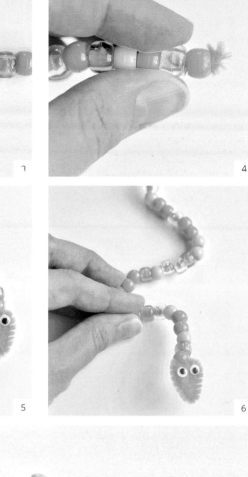

Craft Stick Camping Family

THESE CRAFT STICK PEOPLE are so simple to make, and they make me smile every time I look at them! The hair is just so fun to make and really makes this creation come to life.

WASHI TAPE IS such an awesome low-mess craft material! You can make instant clothes in all sorts of designs and colors without needing to color or paint anything. This crew of campers is dressed for a hot summer day outdoors, but maybe yours will be dressed for a party? Or a fashion show? What outfits will you choose for your little family?

MATERIALS
- 1 large craft stick (the size of a tongue depressor)
- Washi tape
- Yarn

TOOLS
- Scissors
- Washable markers (black and red)
- Crafter's tape

STEP 1: Cut the craft stick in half using sharp scissors.

STEP 2: Draw a happy little face on the rounded end of the craft stick using washable markers.

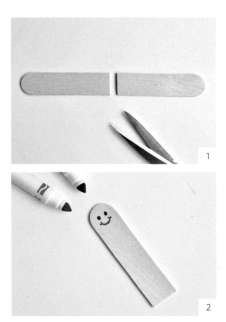

STEP 3: Cut a piece of washi tape, just long enough to wrap around the entire craft stick. Press the front of the craft stick into the middle of the washi tape, just below the face. Wrap the edges of the washi tape around the craft stick and press them onto the back.

STEP 4: Add 2 or 3 more pieces of washi tape with at least 2 different patterns, carefully lining up the edges as you go and pressing the ends onto the back of the craft stick.

STEP 5: Draw buttons on the top washi tape pattern with black washable marker, and pockets and a line down the middle of the bottom washi tape pattern to make shorts.

Then draw simple legs and shoes on the craft stick below.

STEP 6: Wind the yarn around 3 or 4 of your fingers about 10 times. Cut the yarn leaving about 6 inches (15 cm) at the end.

STEP 7: Wind the yarn end tightly around the middle of the yarn wrapped around your fingers and tie it into a knot. (Pull out your middle finger if you need to). Trim off any extra yarn from the knotted end.

STEP 8: Slide the yarn off your fingers and carefully slide scissors into the yarn loops and cut through the yarn. Repeat for the other side.

STEP 9: Apply crafter's tape to the back of the craft stick and press the yarn hair onto it. Trim the yarn if you want to give the craft stick person a different hair style.

STEP 10: Your craft stick person is complete!

☞ Craft ☜
Stick Tent

LEVEL OF DIFFICULTY 3/5 ✦ PARENTAL SUPERVISION NOT REQUIRED.

MATERIALS
- 4 craft sticks
- 1 piece of scrapbook paper

TOOLS
- White glue
- Scissors
- Crafter's tape

THIS PAPER TENT is so fun and looks just like a classic, old-fashioned tent. All you need are some craft sticks and some colored scrapbook paper, and you're all set to begin your camping adventure! Projects that don't use very many craft materials are super easy to tidy up!

I USED COLORED CRAFT STICKS and scrapbook paper for these tents, but you could easily use plain craft sticks and construction paper instead. Sometimes plain materials are even more fun because you can color them with any design you want when you're finished!

STEP 1: Use white glue to attach 2 of the craft sticks together in an upside down "V" shape, with the ends crossing slightly at the top. Repeat for the other 2 craft sticks. Allow the glue to dry.

STEP 2: Cut out a rectangle from the scrapbook paper about 7 inches (18 cm) long by 5 inches (12.5 cm) wide.

Fold the rectangle in half so that the pattern on the paper is on the outside.

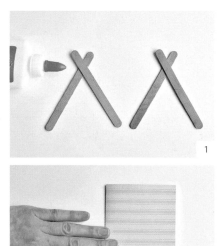

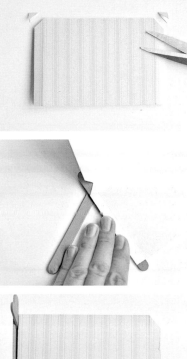

3

4

5

6

7

8

9

10

STEP 3: Open up the fold, then fold in both of the long edges of the rectangle by the width of a craft stick (about ⅜ inch [1 cm]).

STEP 4: Open the folds from Step 3, then fold down the middle again. Trim off the corners of the paper at the folded edge.

STEP 5: Open the folds again. Apply crafter's tape to the narrow folds on the long edge of the rectangle, on the side of the paper with the pattern.

STEP 6: Press the paper with the crafter's tape onto one of the craft sticks so that the fold lines up with the outer edge of the craft stick.

STEP 7: Bend the paper into an upside down "V" shape and press the crafter's tape on the other folded edge onto the other craft stick, again making sure the fold lines up with the outer edge of the craft stick.

STEP 8: Carefully apply crafter's tape to the narrow folds on the other end of the paper.

STEP 9: Press the paper with the crafter's tape onto one of the craft sticks in the second upside down "V" shape. Again, make sure the fold lines up with the outer edge of the craft stick.

Press the last edge onto the last craft stick.

STEP 10: Your craft stick tent is complete!

Paper Roll Frog

FORGET ABOUT PAINTING a toilet paper roll. Just roll up a couple rectangles of construction paper instead! It takes way less time (no need to wait for any paint to dry!) and there's no mess!

THESE PAPER ROLL FROGS are so much fun and they double as a little game. Can your frog catch the fly in his mouth? It's harder than it looks! If you want to make it easy to catch the fly, make the string short. For more of a challenge, make the string longer. Don't worry if it's too long, you can always cut it shorter later.

MATERIALS
- 2 pieces of construction paper (red and green)
- Yarn
- 4 white circle stickers (available at the dollar store or office supplies store)

TOOLS
- Scissors
- Tape
- Stapler
- Crafter's tape
- Washable marker (black)

STEP 1: Cut out 2 rectangles from the construction paper, one red and one green, about 3 inches (7.5 cm) wide by 6 inches (15 cm) long.

STEP 2: Place the red rectangle on top of the green rectangle and roll them into a tube so that the outside is green and the inside is red. Add a long strip of tape to the edge to hold it together.

STEP 3: Cut a piece of yarn about 8 inches (20 cm) long.

STEP 4: Pull the yarn through the paper tube. Pinch the end of the paper tube closed so that the taped edge is on the bottom and the yarn just pokes through the end.

STEP 5: Staple the flattened edge closed, making sure the first staple holds the yarn in place.

STEP 6: Cut out 2 frog arms and 2 frog legs from green construction paper.

STEP 7: Apply crafter's tape to the ends of the arms and legs and press them onto the bottom of the paper roll. (The side of the roll with the taped edge).

STEP 8: Color around the outer edges of 2 white circle stickers with the black washable marker. Color a circle in the center. Peel off the stickers and press them onto the top of the paper roll for the frog's eyes.

STEP 9: Draw a fly shape onto 2 white circle stickers with the black washable marker. Peel off one of the fly stickers and lay it sticky side up on your work surface. Press the end of the yarn onto the sticker.

Peel off the second fly sticker and press it onto the first sticker, lining up the edges, so the sticky sides hold the yarn in place.

STEP 10: Your paper roll frog is complete!

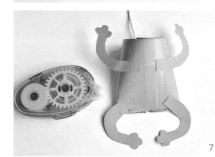

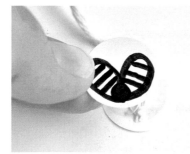

Craft Stick Picnic Table

LEVEL OF DIFFICULTY 3/5 ◆ PARENTAL SUPERVISION
ASK A GROWN UP TO HELP CUT THE CRAFT STICKS IN HALF AND TO HELP WITH THE GLUE GUN.

CRAFT STICKS (I like to call them popsicle sticks) are such a classic craft supply. You can make all sorts of fun objects with them! And as it turns out, it's surprisingly easy to make a picnic table. If you want to simplify this craft, you can leave off the last few steps and make a table instead. It's fun either way!

AND BEST OF ALL, you only need 3 things! It's really easy to keep this one mess-free! You're going to be using up all of the craft sticks, which makes clean up super simple! This craft can definitely be made using white glue instead of a glue gun. If you use white glue, you can follow the exact same steps, you'll just have to wait for the white glue to dry as you go.

STEP 1: Cut one of the craft sticks in half.

STEP 2: Lay 6 craft sticks flat on your work surface and line them up edge to edge so they make a tidy, flat rectangle.

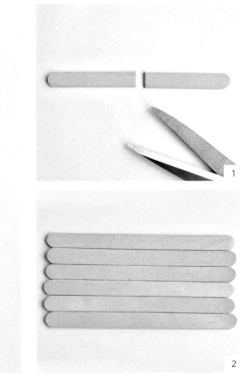

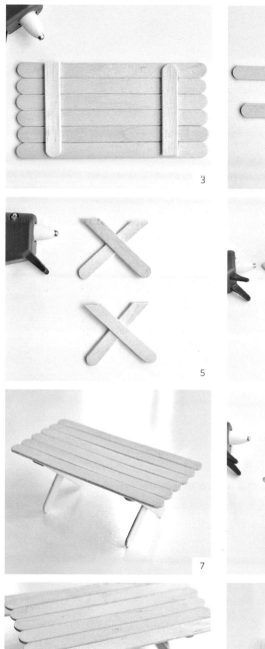

STEP 3: Glue the craft stick halves from Step 1 about ¾ inch (1.9 cm) from the short 2 edges of the rectangle. (The edges with the rounded craft stick ends.)

STEP 4: Cut 2 craft sticks in half. This time make the cuts at an angle.

STEP 5: Glue the craft stick halves together to make 2 "X" shapes. Make sure the flat edges of the craft sticks line up at the top and make a straight line from one edge to the other.

STEP 6: Use a glue gun to attach the flat edges of the 2 "X" shapes to the 2 craft stick halves on the craft stick rectangle, so the "X" shapes stand straight up.

STEP 7: Flip the table over so it stands up on the "X" shaped legs. If the legs are wobbly, pull them off and adjust them as needed.

If you just want to make a table, rather than a full picnic table, feel free to stop here!

STEP 8: Flip the table upside down. Glue a craft stick to the inside of each of the "X" shaped legs so that they are centered on the "X" and parallel to the table top.

STEP 9: Flip the table right side up so there are 2 craft stick ends coming out towards you. Glue 2 craft sticks, edge to edge, on top of the craft stick ends to make the bench seat for the picnic table. Turn the picnic table to the other side and repeat with the last 2 craft sticks.

STEP 10: Your craft stick picnic table is complete!

Easy Paper Cone Trees

LEVEL OF DIFFICULTY 2/5 ✦ PARENTAL SUPERVISION NOT REQUIRED.

THESE PAPER CONE TREES are so simple to make. You'll have your own forest of trees in no time! I used scrapbook paper because I love the texture, but you can easily make this craft with construction paper as well. One circle of paper can make 3 trees!

USING A PEN OR PENCIL to draw patterns on your crafts is a great way to add some low-mess texture and style to your craft projects! Look around the house for a large round object to trace to make the circle shape. I used the lid from a large pot, but you can use a large plate, a round trash can or a compass tool if you have one.

STEP 1: Trace around the edge of a large round lid on the green scrapbook paper, then cut out the circle shape.

STEP 2: Find the middle of the circle and draw a small, wavy circle around the middle with the black gel pen.

Draw another wavy circle about 1 inch (2.5 cm) from the first circle. And another wavy circle 1 inch (2.5 cm) from the second circle.

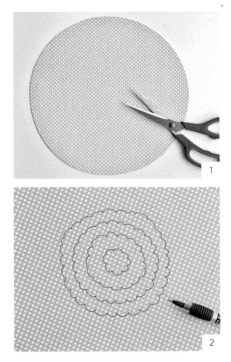

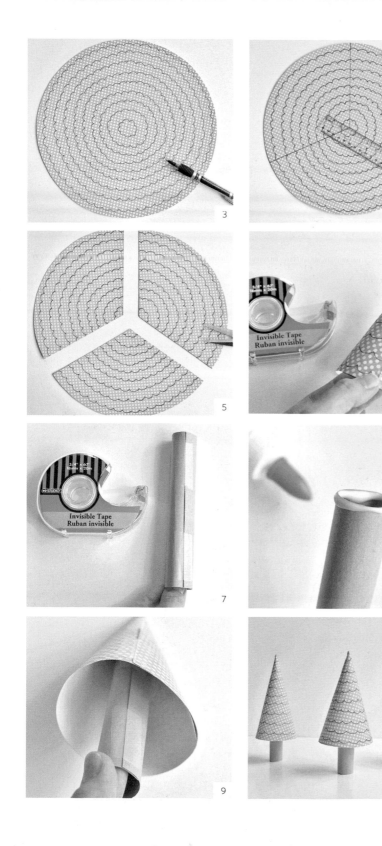

STEP 3: Keep drawing wavy circles, about 1 inch (2.5 cm) from each other until you get to the outside edge of the circle.

STEP 4: Use a ruler to draw lines from the outer edge of the circle to the middle of the circle, dividing it into equal thirds. (It doesn't have to be perfect).

STEP 5: Cut along the lines. Each third of the circle can be used to make a tree.

STEP 6: Roll one piece of the circle into a cone shape. Add tape to the edge on the outside and inside of the cone to hold it together. Repeat for the other 2 pieces of the circle so you end up with 3 cones.

STEP 7: Cut out 3 rectangles from the brown construction paper, about 2½ inches (6.5 cm) wide by 5 inches (12.5 cm) long.

Roll one of the rectangles into a tube shape and tape the edge to hold it together. Repeat for the other 2 rectangles so you end up with 3 tube shapes.

STEP 8: Squeeze a line of white glue around the edge of one end of the tube.

STEP 9: Stick the glued end of the tube into one of the cones, making sure the taped edges line up at the back. Repeat for the other 2 trees. Set the trees upright and allow them to dry.

STEP 10: Your easy paper cone trees are complete.

Simple Quilled ꩜ Ladybug ꩜

LEVEL OF DIFFICULTY 2/5 ◆ PARENTAL SUPERVISION NOT REQUIRED.

LADYBUGS ARE ONE OF MY FAVORITE ANIMALS TO CREATE. I love the simple shape and colors and how they always end up looking cute. This quilled ladybug is super simple to make and it's a great introduction to the art of quilling. There's barely any scraps when you make these tiny little creatures, so cleaning up is simple!

PAPER QUILLING IS A CRAFT where you take long strips of paper, roll them up tightly and combine a bunch of rolled pieces together to make different shapes. You can make hearts, flowers, trees, animals or anything else you can dream up.

MATERIALS
- 2 pieces of construction paper (red and green)
- Toothpick
- 2 small googly eyes
- 1 small pom pom (black)

TOOLS
- Scissors
- Crafter's tape
- Washable markers (green and black)

STEP 1: Cut a long strip of red construction paper, about ½ inch (1.3 cm) wide.

STEP 2: Bend the end of the strip around the toothpick. Roll the paper tightly until you get to the end of the paper strip.

3

4

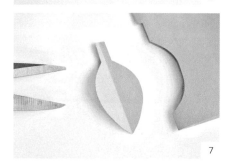

5

6

7

8

9

10

STEP 3: Slide the paper off the toothpick and let the spiral loosen a bit. Apply crafter's tape to the inside end of the red strip and press it down on the spiral to hold it in place.

STEP 4: Draw the ladybug's dots on the outside of the spiral with the black washable marker.

STEP 5: Apply crafter's tape to the back of the googly eyes and press them onto the pom pom.

STEP 6: Apply a small square of crafter's tape to the paper spiral. Gently press the pom pom head onto the spiral ladybug body.

STEP 7: Fold the edge of the green construction paper over by about 2 inches (5 cm). Cut out a leaf shape on the fold.

STEP 8: Draw lines on the leaf using the green washable marker.

STEP 9: Apply a small square of crafter's tape to the middle of the top of the leaf. Gently press the ladybug onto the leaf.

STEP 10: Your simple quilled ladybug is complete!

Chapter 9

Fairy Tale

DRESS UP

Magic mirror, magic mirror (page 172), who do you see? I see kings (page 160) and unicorns (page 170) and woodland creatures (page 166)! It's so much fun to dress up! Practice your magic wand (page 164) waving skills and your very best rhymes for some magic spells. You'll be conjuring up a magic potion or two (page 162).

⁑ LOW-MESS TIP: CHOOSE MATERIALS THAT WILL PERFORM DOUBLE DUTY ⁑

If you want to keep your crafts low-mess, try to find materials that can do two or more things. For example, washi tape can add patterns to your crafts while holding them together. And in the Jewelled Ribbon Necklace in this chapter (page 168), the glue from the hot glue gun is holding the gem in place, but it also gives it some awesome style.

My very favorite double duty craft material is self-adhesive, sparkly craft foam. It has the glitter built right into it, so there's no need to worry about adding your own glitter. When you use self-adhesive craft foam to make the Glittery Magic Wand (page 164) and the Sparkly Unicorn Horn Hat (page 170) in this chapter, you get to skip the glue completely by using the foam's built in sticking power!

Pipe Cleaner Crown (page 160), Magic Potion Bottle (page 162), Glittery Magic Wand (page 164), Woodland Creatue Hairbands (page 166), Jewelled Ribbon Necklace (page 168), Sparkly Unicorn Horn Hat (page 170), Glimmering Cardboard Magic Mirror (page 172), Flower Wreath Headband (page 174)

Pipe Cleaner Crown

LEVEL OF DIFFICULTY 3/5 ♦ PARENTAL SUPERVISION NOT REQUIRED.

MATERIALS
• 7 sparkly pipe cleaners

THESE CROWNS ARE RIDICULOUSLY SIMPLE to make. All you need are pipe cleaners! No glue! Not even scissors! And since you'll be using all of the pipe cleaners, there's zero clean up! How easy is that!?

I USED SPARKLY PIPE CLEANERS for these ones, but you can make colorful crowns from regular pipe cleaners too. When you've mastered this method for making the crowns, try to switch things up. Can you think of any other ways to bend the pipe cleaners to make a fun crown shape? How does it look when you curve the points? What happens if you overlap them at the bottom?

STEP 1: Cross the ends of 2 pipe cleaners by about 1 inch (2.5 cm).

STEP 2: Join the 2 pipe cleaners together by tightly wrapping the 1 inch (2.5 cm) ends around the main pipe cleaner to make one straight, extra long pipe cleaner; set it aside.

STEP 3: Cross another pipe cleaner about 1 inch (2.5 cm) from the middle. Twist the point where the pipe cleaners cross twice to hold it in place. You'll end up with an upside down "V" shape with a loop on the top.

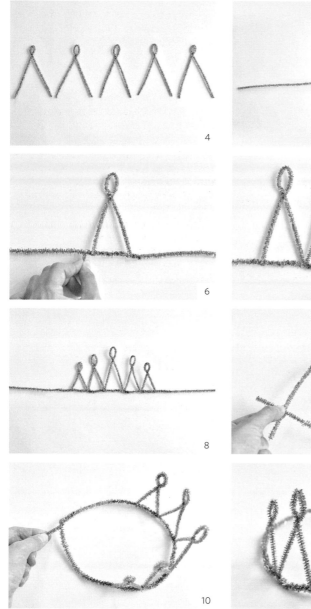

STEP 4: Repeat for the remaining 4 pipe cleaners. You'll end up with 5 looped, upside down "V" shapes.

STEP 5: Place one of the upside down "V" shapes on the middle of the extra long pipe cleaner so that the ends cross over the straight pipe cleaner by about 1 inch (2.5 cm).

STEP 6: Wrap the ends tightly around the long pipe cleaner to hold the upside down "V" shape in place.

STEP 7: Place a second upside down "V" shape right beside the first one, this time with the ends overlapping the extra long pipe cleaner by about 2 inches (5 cm), so the top loop is lower than the first one. Wrap the ends tightly around the long pipe cleaner to hold the second upside down "V" shape in place.

Repeat for a third upside down "V" shape, this time with the ends overlapping the extra long pipe cleaner about about 3 inches (7.5 cm).

STEP 8: Repeat Step 7 with the last two "V" shapes on the other side. Your crown should have 5 points, with the tallest point in the middle and lowest points on the outside.

STEP 9: Take the ends of the extra long pipe cleaner and cross them by about 1 inch (2.5 cm).

STEP 10: Tightly wrap the ends together to make a circle shape. The circle should sit on the top of your head like a crown, so adjust the size if you need to.

STEP 11: Your pipe cleaner crown is complete!

Magic Potion Bottle

LEVEL OF DIFFICULTY 1/5 ✦ PARENTAL SUPERVISION NOT REQUIRED.

HAVE YOU EVER MADE A SENSORY BOTTLE? This is pretty much the same thing, but in a smaller bottle. Give it a good shake and the confetti and glitter almost seem to stand still. Then it almost seems to defy gravity and the shapes inside the bottle fall down to the bottom, ever so slowly.

ITS ALSO A SUPER FUN PROP to include in your dress up wardrobe. The tiny bottle is the perfect size for an imaginary potion! Be sure to make your magic potion on the kitchen or bathroom counter. If you accidentally spill a few drops of water or soap it's pretty simple to clean it up with a cloth or paper towel. And the counters will be cleaner when you're done!

STEP 1: Carefully pour some glitter and/or confetti into the plastic bottle. Pour enough to cover the bottom, but don't fill the bottle by more than ¼ inch (0.6 cm).

STEP 2: Add warm water to the plastic bottle, filling it until the bottle is about ⅓ full.

3

4

STEP 3: Fill the rest of the bottle with clear dish soap. Add as much dish soap as you can without making it overflow. You can even use colored dish soap if you like!

STEP 4: Screw the cap on tightly and rinse the bottle under running water to wash off any soap that might have dripped out. Feel free to glue the cap onto the bottle if there are little hands around that might open it.

STEP 5: Give the bottle a good shake to mix the water and the dish soap. If the glitter moves too slowly, pour a bit of the soap into the sink and add more water.

STEP 6: Your magic potion bottle is complete!

5

6

Glittery Magic Wand

LEVEL OF DIFFICULTY 3/5 ✦ PARENTAL SUPERVISION
ASK A GROWN UP TO HELP WITH CURLING THE RIBBON.

DON'T FORGET ABOUT COOKIE CUTTERS when you're making your crafts! They're amazing when you need a bit of help with making difficult shapes. You can trace around the shape of cookie cutters, wrap pipe cleaners around them to make pipe cleaner shapes or even paint with them! We traced ours to make a perfect star shape for these magic wands.

THERE'S NO NEED TO WORRY about tipping over any jars of glitter here, the glitter foam is packed with built-in glitter! And since it's self-adhesive craft foam, you don't even need glue to hold it together. Any time your craft materials can do double duty (in this case, built-in glitter and stickiness) it helps reduce the mess.

MATERIALS
- 1 sheet of sparkly, self-adhesive craft foam
- Star-shaped cookie cutter
- Paper drinking straw
- Thin gift wrapping ribbon
- 3 small sticker rhinestones

TOOLS
- Pencil
- Scissors

STEP 1: On the back of the sparkly craft foam, trace around the outside of the star shaped cookie cutter. Repeat to make 2 star shapes.

STEP 2: Cut out each of the star shapes.

3

4

STEP 3: Peel off the backing from one of the craft foam stars and place the star sticky side up on your work surface. Gently press the end of the paper drinking straw onto the sticky star so that there is at least 1 inch (2.5 cm) of straw on the sticky part.

STEP 4: Cut out 3 long pieces of thin gift wrapping ribbon. Place the ends of each ribbon onto the sticky star so that there's at least 1 inch (2.5 cm) of ribbon on the sticky part. Space the ribbons evenly beside each other.

STEP 5: Peel off the backing from the other craft foam star. Carefully line up the points of the star and press the sticky sides together.

STEP 6: Press the sticker rhinestones onto the paper drinking straw, evenly spaced right below the star.

5

6

STEP 7: Curl each of the ribbons by dragging the ribbon tightly across one edge of the scissors. Start with the scissors close to the star and work your way outwards to the end of the ribbon.

STEP 8: Your glittery magic wand is complete!

7

8

Woodland Creature Hairbands

LEVEL OF DIFFICULTY 3/5 ✦ PARENTAL SUPERVISION
ASK A GROWN UP TO HELP WITH THE GLUE GUN.

MATERIALS
- 1 scrap of thick paper
- 2 sheets of felt (2 different colors works best)
- 1 hairband

TOOLS
- Scissors
- Gel pen
- Low-temperature glue gun

MY DAUGHTER GOT a mouse hairband as a birthday party favour once and I thought it was absolutely brilliant! Some of the kids even wore them to school in the months that followed, they were just so cute!

THESE WOODLAND CREATURE HAIRBANDS are simple to make, there's no sewing required and there's barely any scraps—which means cleaning up is easy! Try making a bunny, fox, mouse, owl, deer, bear or even a frog hairband. You can make them in browns and grays, or you can use bright and bold colors. It's completely up to you!

STEP 1: Trace a circle shape (or any other creature ear shape!) onto the scrap of thick paper. Make sure you leave a tab at the bottom, about ¼ inch (0.6 cm) long. This will leave room to wrap it around the hairband later. Cut out the ear shape from the paper.

Fold one end of the felt up by about 3 inches (7.5 cm). Place the flat tab of the ear shape on the fold in the felt. Use a gel pen to trace around the edge of the ear shape. Repeat to make a second ear shape.

STEP 2: Cut out the ear shapes over the fold through the 2 layers of felt.

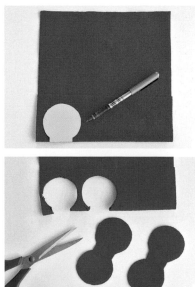

3

4

5

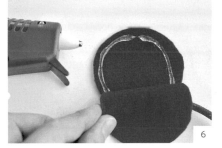

6

7

8

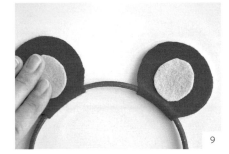

9

10

STEP 3: Position the ears on the hairband. Make sure the middle tab is centered underneath the hairband. Add a line of glue from the glue gun on the straight tab part of the felt.

STEP 4: Pull the ear up and over the hair band, lining up the edges of the ear. Press the felt onto the hairband to hold the glue in place.

STEP 5: Open up the 2 pieces of felt and add a line of hot glue to the top of the hairband. Make sure you only add glue where the felt is going to cover the hairband. Line up the edges of the felt again, and press along the top of the hairband where the glue was.

STEP 6: Add a line of hot glue around the inside edge of one side of the felt. Make sure the glue is at least ¼ inch (0.6 cm) from the edge so it doesn't leak out. Line up the edges of the felt and gently press them together over the glue.

STEP 7: Repeat Step 3 to Step 6 for the other ear.

STEP 8: Cut out two ovals from the second color of felt. Add a line of hot glue around the edge of the oval, at least ¼ inch (0.6 cm) from the edge.

STEP 9: Position the smaller felt oval onto the felt ear and gently press it down to hold the glue in place. Repeat for the second felt oval.

STEP 10: Your woodland creature hairband is complete!

Jewelled Ribbon
✦ Necklace ✦

LEVEL OF DIFFICULTY 1/5 ✦ PARENTAL SUPERVISION
ASK A GROWN UP TO HELP WITH THE GLUE GUN.

WE'VE ALL MADE NECKLACES from beads and baubles, but have you ever made your own necklace pendants from hot glue and rhinestones? They are so simple, and they look so pretty when they're done! The hot glue holding the rhinestone surrounds the gem and almost makes it look like it was professionally set in place.

WHEN YOU'RE MAKING YOUR CRAFTS, remember to choose bright, colorful and/or sparkly craft supplies that look amazing on their own, whenever you can. When you don't need any extra glitter, markers or decorations it's easy to keep the mess to a minimum.

MATERIALS
- 1 piece of craft foam
- 1 large rhinestone
- Ribbon

TOOLS
- Scissors
- Single hole punch
- Low-temperature glue gun

STEP 1: Cut out a small rectangle from the craft foam, making it about twice as big as your rhinestone. Trim around the edges of the rectangle to turn it into an oval shape.

STEP 2: Punch a hole in the top of the oval with a single hole punch.

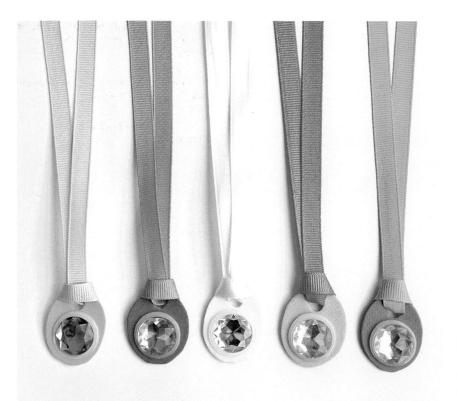

3

STEP 3: Add a large glob of glue from the glue gun to the oval shape, centered between the bottom edge of the oval and the punched hole.

4

STEP 4: Carefully press the rhinestone onto the glob of glue, letting the glue leak out from underneath the gem. Allow the hot glue to cool for about 5 to 10 minutes, or until it's completely dry.

STEP 5: Cut a piece of ribbon about 24 inches (61 cm) long.

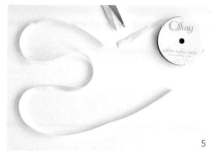

5

6

STEP 6: Fold the ribbon in half and carefully push the fold through the hole in the craft foam, going from the front towards the back. Pull the ribbon through by about 1 inch (2.5 cm).

STEP 7: Bring the 2 ends of the ribbon together and push them through the loop of ribbon sticking out from the back of the craft foam.

7

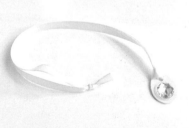

8

STEP 8: Pull the ribbon all the way through and carefully tighten the loop against the top of the oval.

STEP 9: Tie the 2 ends of the ribbon together in a knot. Trim the ends if you need to.

STEP 10: Your jewelled ribbon necklace is complete!

9

10

Sparkly Unicorn Horn Hat

LEVEL OF DIFFICULTY 3/5 + PARENTAL SUPERVISION NOT REQUIRED.

THE MYSTICAL UNICORN! Do you know anyone who loves them? It's super easy to make your own unicorn horn from self-adhesive craft foam and ribbon. It's easy to keep the mess down when your craft supplies have stickiness built right into them. You get to skip the glue completely for this one!

THESE UNICORN HORNS also make an awesome birthday party favour! (Did you notice that they are also very similar to party hats?) Place the horn on your head, tie the ribbon under your chin and it's an instant transformation!

MATERIALS
- 1 piece of sparkly, self-adhesive craft foam
- Thin ribbon
- Thick ribbon

TOOLS
- Scissors

STEP 1: Cut out a pie-shaped piece of craft foam, about 7 inches (18 cm) long on the straight edges and 6½ inches (16.5 cm) wide on the curved end (or a similar size that fits on your piece of craft foam).

STEP 2: Trim off ½ inch (1.3 cm) from the point of the pie shape.

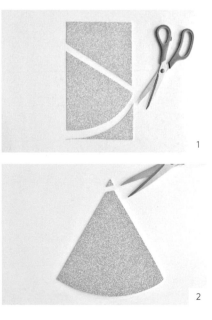

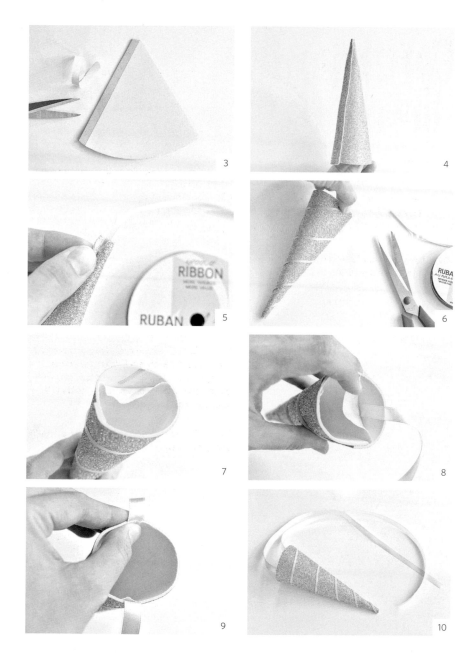

STEP 3: Cut off about ½ inch (1.3 cm) of the paper backing from one edge of the craft foam, leaving about ½ inch (1.3 cm) of the sticky part showing.

STEP 4: Roll the craft foam into a cone shape. Use the sticky inside edge of the foam to hold the shape together. If the bottom edges don't meet perfectly, trim the bottom edge of the cone and make sure it can stand straight up.

STEP 5: Take the end of the thin ribbon and carefully push it into the point of the cone. Open the point of the cone if you need to and make sure you press it tightly closed again to keep the ribbon in place.

STEP 6: Wrap the thin ribbon around the cone several times, evenly spacing the ribbon as you work your way from the point down to the bottom of the cone. Cut the ribbon, leaving at least 1 inch (2.5 cm) of extra ribbon at the bottom.

STEP 7: Carefully peel back a small portion of the self-adhesive backing and press the ribbon onto the sticky part. Push the backing back in place over the ribbon.

STEP 8: Cut 2 pieces of the thicker ribbon, about 20 inches (51 cm) long each. Carefully peel back a small portion of the self-adhseive backing and press about 1 inch (2.5 cm) of the thicker ribbon onto the sticky part of the foam.

STEP 9: Push the paper backing back in place over the ribbon.

Repeat Step 8 and 9 with the other piece of ribbon on the opposite side of the cone.

STEP 10: Your sparkly unicorn horn hat is complete!

Glimmering Cardboard
Magic Mirror ♡

LEVEL OF DIFFICULTY 3/5 ✦ PARENTAL SUPERVISION NOT REQUIRED.

WHAT DO YOU SEE IN YOUR MAGIC MIRROR? Does it show you magical things happening in another world? Does it show you what your prince or princess is doing? Every fairy tale story can use a magic mirror, and it's so easy to make your own from cardboard and aluminum foil.

WHY COVER THE CARDBOARD in glue and glitter when you can trace the shape and use a piece of glittering craft foam instead?! You'll need a small amount of white glue for this craft to attach the rhinestones, but if you remember to only add a small amount at a time, there will be no drips and no mess.

MATERIALS
- 1 piece of cardboard, about 6"x10" (15 x 25 cm) (a cardboard box works well)
- 1 piece of sparkly self-adhesive craft foam
- 1 small piece of aluminum foil
- Rhinestones
- Ribbon

TOOLS
- Pencil
- Scissors
- Crafter's tape
- White glue

STEP 1: Draw the shape of a handheld mirror onto the piece of cardboard.

STEP 2: Cut out the cardboard mirror shape. Place the shape on the back of the craft foam and trace around the mirror shape.

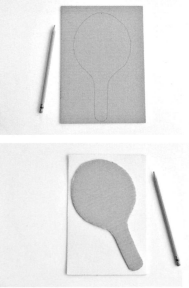

3

4

5

6

7

8

9

10

STEP 3: Cut out the craft foam mirror shape. Fold the middle of the craft foam mirror just enough to make a small cut in it with scissors. Poke the scissors through the hole and cut out an oval from the middle of the craft foam mirror.

STEP 4: Add a few lines of crafter's tape to the cardboard mirror.

STEP 5: Cut out an oval shape from the aluminum foil a little bit larger than the oval opening in the foam mirror shape.

Lay the aluminum foil oval on the cardboard mirror, being careful not to wrinkle it, and gently press it onto the crafter's tape.

STEP 6: Peel off the adhesive backing from the craft foam mirror shape. Line up the edges and press it onto the cardboard mirror.

STEP 7: Add white glue to the back of the rhinestones and press them onto the sparkly craft foam.

STEP 8: Continue gluing on rhinestones until you've gone around the entire oval surrounding the aluminum foil.

STEP 9: Cut out a piece of ribbon, about 12 inches (30.5 cm) long and tie it in a bow around the handle of your mirror.

STEP 10: Your glimmering cardboard magic mirror is complete!

HINT: If you want a broken mirror, just crinkle up the aluminum foil before you attach it to the cardboard. You could even make your mirror reversible so it's shiny on one side and crinkly broken on the other side!

Flower Wreath
Headband

LEVEL OF DIFFICULTY 2/5 ◆ PARENTAL SUPERVISION
ASK A GROWN UP TO HELP WITH THE GLUE GUN.

DOESN'T IT SEEM LIKE the fairest and kindest characters always have a flower wreath in their hair? The villains very rarely get to wear something so beautiful. These headbands are so pretty and they're amazingly simple to make!

THIS IS A FANTASTIC LOW-MESS CRAFT that only uses a handful of materials. Add a dot of hot glue to the flower, press it onto the elastic and repeat—it's so easy! Do you have any extra flowers left over? Tape a few together and tie a ribbon around the stems to make a bouquet to go with your headband.

MATERIALS

- ½" (1.3 cm) wide elastic (available at the craft store or fabric store)
- Fabric flowers and leaves, different sizes and colors
- Wide ribbon

TOOLS

- Scissors
- Low-temperature glue gun

STEP 1: Cut a piece of the wide elastic to be about 24 inches (61 cm) long.

STEP 2: Pull the fabric flowers off from the stems. Trim off the plastic piece at the back of the flowers so the flowers will lay flat.

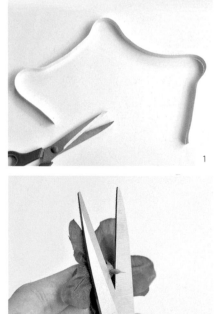

3

5

7

9

4

6

8

10

STEP 3: Decide where the largest fabric flower is going to be placed on the elastic band. It looks best if it's positioned about ⅓ from the end.

STEP 4: Add a small glob of glue from the glue gun to the back of the largest fabric flower.

STEP 5: Carefully press the glue onto the wide elastic.

STEP 6: Continue gluing on flowers until there's only about 3 inches (7.5 cm) or 4 inches (10 cm) of the wide elastic showing at each end. This will depend on the size of your head—make sure the flowers go all the way around your head.

Cut fabric leaves from the stems (if you have them) and glue them between some of the flowers to fill in any gaps.

STEP 7: Tie the ends of the elastic into a double knot. Test the size on your head and adjust it if you need to. Pull the ends to make the knot tight, then add some hot glue to the knot to keep it from coming apart. Trim off any extra elastic.

STEP 8: Cut 2 long pieces of ribbon, about 24 inches (61 cm) each. Cut the ends at an angle.

STEP 9: Find the middle of the ribbons and tie them around the knot in the elastic at the back of the headband. You should end up with 4 long pieces of equal length ribbon dangling from the back.

STEP 10: Your flower wreath headband is complete!

HINT: Look for inexpensive and colorful fabric flowers at the dollar store or craft store. Sometimes you can even find them at a second hand store.

LIST OF SUPPLIES FOR EACH CHAPTER

SUPPLIES FOR CHAPTER 1
MY SECRET GARDEN

- Craft sticks (colored and/or plain)
- Small buttons (2 or 3)
- Construction paper (assorted colors)
- Thick paper (assorted colors)
- Pipe cleaners (regular and sparkly)
- Clothespins (2 or 3)
- Googly eyes (small)
- Sticker rhinestones (assorted colors and sizes)
- Sparkly pom poms (assorted colors and sizes)
- Battery operated tea lights (2 or 3)
- Wine corks (2 or 3)
- Fabric flower daisy
- 1 inch (2.5 cm) wooden bead (available at the craft store or from Amazon.com)
- Smooth rocks (medium and small, 2 or 3 each)
- Red and white "multi-surface" acrylic paint

You'll also need these standard craft supplies and household items.
- White glue
- Low-temperature glue gun
- Glue stick
- Crafter's tape
- Tape
- Pencil
- Washable markers
- Paint brushes
- Scissors
- Toothpick
- Disposable dinner plate

SUPPLIES FOR CHAPTER 2
UNDER THE SEA

- Pipe cleaners (assorted colors)
- Sparkly self-adhesive craft foam (green)
- Googly eyes (small, medium and large)
- Thick paper (assorted colors)
- Clothespins (2 or 3)
- Borax (available at the supermarket in the laundry section)
- Craft sticks (2 or 3)
- Thin (3/8-inch [1-cm] wide) ribbon
- Thick (5/8-inch [1.6-cm] wide) ribbon
- Blue plastic cups (2 or 3)
- Cupcake liners (2 to 4)
- Gift wrapping ribbon
- Smooth rocks (2 or 3)
- Liquid chalk markers (assorted colors)
- Pom poms (green, 2 or 3)
- Plastic spoons (2 or 3)

You'll also need these standard craft supplies and household items.
- Glue stick
- Crafter's tape
- Pencil
- Washable markers
- Scissors
- Small ruler
- String
- 2-cup (480-mL) mason jar (or any container about that size)

SUPPLIES FOR CHAPTER 3
SUMMER AT THE BEACH

- Sparkly craft foam (1 or 2 colors)
- Self-adhesive craft foam (white and another color or 2)
- Brightly-colored plastic drinking straws (at least 6)
- Red tape (electrical or washi tape)
- Wine corks (at least 3)
- Wooden skewers (4 or 5)
- Pipe cleaners (assorted colors)
- 1 wooden bead (about 3/4 inch [1.9 cm])

- Plastic pony beads (assorted colors)
- Construction paper (assorted colors)
- Tissue paper (1 piece, yellow)
- Glass beads (the kind used to fill vases)
- Googly eyes (small and medium)
- Small plastic craft supply zip bags (about 3 x 2 inches [7.5 x 5 cm])
- Colored baker's twine (or really thin ribbon)
- Washi tape (at least 2 different patterns)
- Yarn (multicolored if possible)
- Seashells (at least 2 matching)
- Acrylic paint (at least one favorite color)
- Disposable dinner plate

You'll also need these standard craft supplies and household items.
- Low-temperature glue gun
- Glue stick
- Crafter's tape
- Masking tape
- Pencil
- Washable markers
- Black gel pen
- Scissors
- Paint brush
- Ruler
- 2 wide elastics (the elastics that hold broccoli together are perfect!)

- "L" shaped hook with a screw end (or a regular screw and a screw driver)
- Small hole punch

SUPPLIES FOR CHAPTER 4 ANIMALS AT THE ZOO
- Construction paper (assorted colors)
- Thick paper (light brown, 1 piece)
- Tissue paper (yellow, 1 piece)
- Pipe cleaners (assorted colors)
- Googly eyes (extra small, small, medium and large)
- Foam ball (slightly larger than the opening in a toilet paper roll)
- Pom poms (yellow, 2 medium, 2 small, 1 very small)
- Foam cups (1 or 2)
- White liquid chalk marker (or white pencil crayon)
- Craft foam (brown, 1 piece)
- Large pom poms (pink, 1 or 2)
- Craft feathers (pink, 2 to 4)
- Craft sticks (4 plain)
- Sparkly self-adhesive craft foam (blue, 1 piece)
- Sticker rhinestones (medium, silver, about 20)

You'll also need these standard craft supplies and household items.
- White glue
- Low-temperature glue gun
- Glue stick
- Tape
- Crafter's tape
- Washable markers

- Pencil
- Scissors
- Toilet paper rolls (at least 3)

SUPPLIES FOR CHAPTER 5 LITTLE MONSTERS PUPPET SHOW
- Colored paper, thick and/ or construction paper (assorted colors)
- Fuzzy socks (1 or 2)
- Curly ribbon pre-made gift wrapping bow (1 or 2)
- Self-adhesive craft foam (red and/or black, 1 piece)
- Pom poms (assorted colors and sizes)
- Sparkly pom poms (1 large, 3 medium)
- Buttons (at least 2)
- Googly eyes (small, medium and large)
- Foam cups
- Craft sticks (at least 3)
- Pipe cleaners (assorted colors)
- Winter gloves (kids size, 1 or 2)
- Scrap of long hair fur (available at the craft store or fabric store)
- Rubber dish glove (green, 1 or 2)
- Craft foam (red and yellow, 1 piece each)
- Foam ball (about 1½ inch (3.8 cm) wide, 1 or 2)
- Yarn
- Craft feathers (2 small)
- 2 glass beads (the kind used to fill vases)
- Ribbon (about ⅜ inch [1 cm])

You'll also need these standard craft supplies and household items.

- Low-temperature glue gun
- Glue stick
- Crafter's tape
- Washable markers
- Black permanent marker
- Pencil
- Craft knife
- Scissors
- Sewing needle
- Thread
- Scrap of cardboard

SUPPLIES FOR CHAPTER 6
ON THE ROAD

- Thick paper (assorted colors)
- Construction paper (assorted colors)
- Shiny wrapping paper (1 small piece)
- Sparkly washi tape (thin)
- Green poster board (1 sheet)
- Black duct tape
- White roll on correction tape
- Large sticker rhinestones (1 red, 3 yellow and 1 green)
- Medium sticker rhinestones (red and white, 2 to 4 each)
- Craft foam (black, 1 piece)
- Mini shampoo bottle (travel size, 1 or 2)
- Red electrical tape
- Pipe cleaners (black, 1 or 2)
- Sparkly foam star stickers (2 to 4)
- Milkshake straw (wider than regular straws)

- Self-adhesive white label (1 or 2)
- Wooden skewers (3 or 4)
- Mini wooden blocks (available at the craft store or dollar store, about 5 or 6)
- White liquid chalk marker
- Tri-fold display board (or a large cardboard box)

You'll also need these standard craft supplies and household items.

- Low-temperature glue gun
- Glue stick
- Crafter's tape
- Tape
- Pencil
- Washable markers
- Single hole punch
- Scissors
- Ruler
- Drinking straws (2 to 4)
- Toilet paper rolls (1 or 2)
- Empty mini candy box (Smarties, or similar size)
- Plastic bottle lid (1 or 2)
- Empty tissue box (1 or 2)
- Label maker (optional)
- Apple sauce pouch lids (at least 4)
- Foam cup (or regular cup for tracing)

SUPPLIES FOR CHAPTER 7
EXPLORING OUTER SPACE

- Wooden peg dolls (available at the craft store or at Amazon.com)
- Paint (assorted colors, including white)

- Gold paint pen
- Colored paper (thick and/or construction paper, assorted colors)
- Foam ball (about 2 inches [5.1 cm] wide)
- Wooden skewers (3 or 4)
- Fine glitter (red, gold and silver)
- Large glitter (gold)
- Mini wooden blocks (available at the craft store or dollar store, at least 4)
- Pipe cleaners (green, 1 or 2)
- Tissue paper (yellow, 1 piece)
- Pom poms (medium, 2 to 4 green)
- Circle stickers (white, 3 to 6)
- Suction cup hooks (2 or 3)
- Black tempera paint (washable)
- Paper dessert plates (1 or 2)
- Clear plastic cups (1 or 2)
- Googly eyes (small and large)
- Polka dot scrapbook paper (1 or 2 sheets)
- Sparkly star stickers (about 100)

You'll also need these standard craft supplies and household items.

- White glue
- Low-temperature glue gun
- Glue stick
- Crafter's tape
- Tape
- Masking tape
- Washable markers
- Pencil

- Paint brush
- Paper plate
- Scissors
- Craft knife
- Old and unneeded CD or DVD
- Toilet paper rolls (1 or 2)
- Empty plastic bottle (green, 1 or 2)
- Round plastic lid (from a yogurt or sour cream container, 2 or 3)
- Toothpick
- Thread
- Baking soda

SUPPLIES FOR CHAPTER 8
LETS GO CAMPING

- Craft sticks (colored and plain)
- Scrapbook paper (fun tent colors and green pattern)
- Pipe cleaners (assorted colors)
- Plastic pony beads (assorted colors)
- Googly eyes (small)
- Large craft sticks (the size of a tongue depressor, 2 or 3)
- Washi tape (2 or 3 different patterns)
- Yarn
- Construction paper (assorted colors)
- Tiny elastics (1 or 2)
- White circle stickers (at least 4)
- Tissue paper (red, orange and yellow, 1 piece each)

- Battery operated tea lights (1 or 2)
- Small pom poms (white and black, 1 or 2 each)
- Wooden skewer
- Circle stickers (white)

You'll also need these standard craft supplies and household items.

- White glue
- Low-temperature glue gun
- Crafter's tape
- Tape
- Washable markers
- Pencil
- Black gel pen
- Scissors
- Ruler
- Stapler
- Toothpicks

SUPPLIES FOR CHAPTER 9
FAIRY TALE DRESS UP

- Sparkly pipe cleaners (gold, at least 7)
- Sparkly, self-adhesive craft foam (several different colors, at least 3 or 4 pieces)
- Thin gift wrapping ribbon
- Paper drinking straws (1 or 2)
- Sticker rhinestones (small, 3 to 6)
- Felt (at least 2 different colors, 1 piece each)
- Hairband (1 or 2)
- Craft foam (2 or 3 different colors, 1 piece each)
- Large rhinestones (assorted colors)

- Ribbon (approximately ⅜ inch [1 cm] wide and ⅛ inch [0.3 cm] wide)
- Ribbon (green, 1 inch [2.5 cm] wide)
- Confetti and/or large glitter
- Travel size clear plastic bottle (1 or 2)
- Fabric flowers and leaves (different sizes and colors)
- ½ inch (1.3 cm) wide elastic (available at the craft store or fabric store)

You'll also need these standard craft supplies and household items.

- White glue
- Low-temperature glue gun
- Crafter's tape
- Pencil
- Black gel pen
- Scissors
- Single hole punch
- Star shaped cookie cutter
- Clear liquid dish soap
- Scrap from a cardboard box
- Aluminum foil

Folded Ribbon Fish (page 40)

ACKNOWLEDGMENTS

I am so grateful to Lauren Knowles and Page Street Publishing for bringing this book to life. Thank you for all your help, encouragement and for taking a chance on me!

A huge thank you to my husband, Jason Chapman, for all his love and support while I photographed and wrote this book. I appreciate all of your help and the sacrifices you made! Thank you for helping me troubleshoot my craft problems, lending an extra set of hands and eyes whenever I needed them and for keeping the kids from running away with my projects. I couldn't have done it without you!

Last but not least, thank you to my awesome kids and hand models, Leah, Kate and Benjamin. You did a fantastic job testing out the crafts in this book and you had extraordinary patience watching me photograph all the fun things that you weren't allowed to touch. I promise that now that the book is done you can start using my craft supplies and finally play with all the amazing things we made together!

Paper Roll Fairy House (page 16)

ABOUT THE AUTHOR

Debbie lives in London, Ontario, Canada with her husband Jason and her three young children. She worked as an engineer for almost 8 years before leaving her job to follow her love of cooking, crafting and creating things.

When she's not cleaning up after her three little mess-makers she's busy making things, photographing them and writing on her blog, One Little Project. She regularly posts step-by-step photo tutorials of fun kids crafts, easy family recipes, cute holiday treats and more!

To see more of her fun craft ideas visit onelittleproject.com.

INDEX

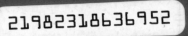